LEARNING GOLF: THE LYLE WAY

LEARNING GOLF: THE LYLE WAY

THE SURE AND SIMPLE WAY TO PLAY THE GAME

BY

SANDY LYLE

1985 BRITISH OPEN CHAMPION AND THREE-TIME LEADING MONEY WINNER ON THE PGA EUROPEAN TOUR

WITH

JOHN ANDRISANI

1817

Harper & Row, Publishers, New York
Grand Rapids, Philadelphia, St. Louis, San Francisco
London, Singapore, Sydney, Tokyo

Illustrations and photographs by Ken Lewis
Photographs on pages 182 and 183 by Lawrence Levy

This book was originally published in 1986 in Great Britain by Hodder and Stoughton Limited. It is reprinted here by arrangement with Hodder and Stoughton Limited.

FIRST U.S. EDITION

LIBRARY OF CONGRESS CATALOG CARD NUMBER 88-45897
ISBN 0-06-016082-9

89 90 91 92 93 RRD 10 9 8 7 6 5 4 3 2 1

CONTENTS

FOREWORD

BY ALEX LYLE

Longtime professional at Hawkstone Park Golf Club, Shropshire, England, and Sandy Lyle's original and most faithful teacher

T he final 18 holes of the 1985 British Open Championship were nerve-racking, but wonderfully exciting. Watching Sandy struggle at the start, slip back into contention and then secure victory by sinking two big birdie putts down the home stretch brought happy tears to my eyes.

I knew how hard my son had worked to capture this dream. To see his dream come true was fantastic for our family, Sandy's friends, and fans, like you.

While viewing the final round on television, and sipping several Whiskies to tame the tension and twitches, a golfing lifetime with Sandy played before my eyes!

I remembered the day I sized up Sandy with an old cut-down wooden club, so he could play around on the practice tee of our home course, Hawkstone Park.

Then, seeing the gleam in Sandy's eyes, not so long after, as he played the course for the first time, at the age of four.

I remembered sharing Sandy's grief and glory during those growing golfing days, when he found out that the game, like life, seesaws.

And that spring afternoon, when Sandy stepped into our sitting room to make a so-called surprise announcement: "Dad, one day, I want to become a professional golfer." I admit I wasn't shocked by this news. However, the statement was an ambitious one for a boy of ten, who had only started to play *seriously* at the age of eight.

More walks through memory lane, as I recalled summers past, and Sandy's frequent morning and evening practice sessions. From our kitchen window, I used to peer through binoculars, watching closely to see if Sandy was paying attention to my advice: "tempo, not temper"; "a waltz is better than a quickstep"; and "keep your head".

Glancing back to the telly, I thought, "By God, Sandy has always been a work-horse, he deserves to win this British Open".

Then, back to another classic scene in my mental movie, that historic day in 1969, when Sandy sat in the stands surrounding the 18th green at

Royal Lytham & St Annes, witnessing Tony Jacklin's British Open win. From that moment onward, Sandy started dreaming of one day being the "Open" champion.

Now, I was standing next to Sandy, as he prepared to tee off in his first Carris Trophy, a major amateur event on our side of the Atlantic. I told him to take a couple of deep breaths, to relax. When he turned to me and said, "Dad, you're more nervous than I am," I knew he had an essential quality of a champion – "courage". Sandy finished third, an excellent effort, I thought, for a first-time starter. My son didn't think so. He wasn't happy until he took home the Trophy in 1975.

One memory after another, some muddled, most crystal clear, played before me. The time, in 1974, when Sandy qualified for the Open at Royal Lytham, while still an amateur, and just missed making it into the final round; the day, in 1975, when he won the first of two English Amateur Stroke Play titles; the day, in 1977, when he was selected for the Walker Cup squad. The list went on and on.

Deep feelings, repressed for many years, rose to the surface. (For so long, I had to stand on middle ground. I didn't want to praise Sandy too much, for fear that he would get overconfident and collapse. So, I told him to take his golf step-by-step, and that if he kept improving, maybe one day he would be able to make a living from tournament golf.)

My mind switched back to the telly. I knew that Sandy was aware of one fact: there is a big difference between winning a tournament and winning an Open. Watching Sandy play the 14th hole, I wanted to fly inside the television, pat him on the back, and say, "Come on, my son, I know you can do it." And by God, he did, sinking a 45-foot birdie putt. But he had a few holes to play. The round was too full of suspense for me, so I returned to those big and little moments, mixed in my memory.

The day Sandy won the PGA European Tour Qualifying School came to mind. After that event, Sandy told me that he only teed off with the driver four times in 72 holes. "Why?" I asked him. "Because I heard so many drives bouncing off trees." This statement of common sense assured me that he had adopted the mature attitude of managing his game.

Many more days flashed before me. Sandy's first year on Tour: he won the Nigerian Open, earned Rookie-of-the-Year honours, but finished 49th on the Order of Merit. He wasn't satisfied, showing me he had the hunger to win big. He proved that straightaway, finishing top of the money list the next two years.

Another memory: Sandy's 1979 European Open win, a big confidence booster, as was his 1984 Kapalua victory in Hawaii, when he beat a major field of American and international players.

Back to the telly. Sandy sank a birdie putt at the 15th hole, clenched his fist, and the look of determination showed on his face. I thought, then, that an Open win was on the cards. As it turned out, I was right!

When I watched Sandy hug the famous Open Championship Trophy, I knew he finally believed, deep down in his heart, that sacrifice and sweat can pay off. Somehow, all along, I knew that Sandy would receive his reward, but I never let him think it would be easy.

There stood my son, the Open champion. Sandy had learned to win the big one. And that's about all a golfing father can ask of a golfing son. One less dream for Sandy, one more memory for me.

During those four days at Royal St George's, Sandy showed me the qualities of a world-class winner: courage, common sense, confidence, patience, persistence, temperament, tenacity, swing tempo, strength, staying power, shotmaking ability, and "killer instinct".

Sandy's performance proved that beneath his quiet exterior is the heart of a lion, a constant quest, a real thirst, for victory. When Sandy's up against it, he knows how to go for the jugular, and that's another mark of a champion.

Since the 1985 British Open, Sandy has truly proven his talents over and over again, particularly by winning the '87 Tournament Players' Championship and Suntory World Match-Play Championship, two prestigious events that many golf aficionados regard as "major" titles. However, Sandy's will-to-win may never have been greater than on the final hole of the '88 Masters, when under tremendous pressure he pulled off an impossible-looking fairway bunker shot that may forever stay in the record books, for it set up a winning birdie putt.

I sure have learned a lot about my son through his golf. But *Learning Golf: The Lyle Way* gave me even more insight into Sandy's character, his imagination, his swing and shotmaking secrets. Over the years, I have taught Sandy a lot about technique, but this book is evidence that he has learned a whole lot on his own. Without giving the book away, or stealing the show, let me give you a sneak preview.

You and I know that every golfer searches for a swing key. What's more, throughout the game's history, thousands of tips have been offered by players and teachers. And without sounding like a know-it-all, I think I have heard just about all of them. *Learning Golf: The Lyle Way*, however, is filled with original tips. And quite honestly, I didn't think there was any such "state of the art" instruction around. Let me show you what I mean.

Sandy compares swing tempo to a musical scale. Picture a singer going through the range of tones: *do, re, me fa, soh, la, te, do.* Imagine each one getting higher, and you'll start to appreciate what Sandy is getting at. He suggests that the old advice, to say "one" as you swing the club up, and "two", as you swing the club down, throws off your timing, because the downswing should be quicker than the backswing. Believe it or not, the downswing only takes about one fifth of a second. While the backswing, from the address position to the top, takes almost one and a half seconds.

Sandy tells you to key on the musical tones – the pitch increasing from *do*, to *re*, to *me*, to *fa*, to *soh*, to *la*, to *te*, and finally, to *do* – so that you get a feel for the swing's speed building up, until the final moment of impact, when the clubface smacks the ball. I am happy to say that this image, and numerous other instructions in this book, are unique, and will help newcomers and experienced players alike. And I'm not saying this because Sandy is my son.

You see, the great thing about golf is that no matter how old or experienced you are, you never stop learning. And I am pleased that Sandy learned this lesson long ago. Otherwise, he could never have written such a first-class book as *Learning Golf: The Lyle Way.*

WRITER'S COMMENTARY

BY JOHN ANDRISANI

In America, during the 1977 Walker Cup Matches, a youngster with an impressive swing, and equally creditable demeanour, caught my eye. His age of nineteen, however, dismissed any thoughts of putting an asterisk alongside his name, for things could transpire down the road, and had done before, to other promising players. Besides, surely his fearless swing was simply youthful lack of inhibition showing its face, and his excellent temperament, the shyness of a teenager.

What would become of this young man once he turned professional and fell victim to the pressure of Tour golf? What would happen to his free-flowing rhythm, once a teacher started dissecting his swing? Would his adherence to sound fundamentals come unstuck, once he was tempted with trendy swing theories? I pondered these thoughts upon leaving Shinnecock Hills.

Three years later, when I settled into a job in England, as assistant-editor for *Golf Illustrated*, I caught up with Sandy Lyle at Hawkstone Park.

He had already won on the professional circuit. His swing still ran as efficiently as a Rolls-Royce and looked as effortless as ever. The only differences I could see in Sandy were that he had put numerous new shots into his repertoire, and had an even keener understanding of what makes a first-class technique tick. The trick to such magic? Sandy's own imaginative powers, plus the swing secrets passed on to him by his father, Alex Lyle.

During my stay at *Golf Illustrated*, Sandy and I had opportunities to tee-it-up together and to talk technique for hours at a time.

Shortly after I moved back to New York, in late 1982, to work as senior editor of instruction at *Golf Magazine*, Sandy arranged, through his agent Mark McCormack, a meeting at Bay Hill, Florida, where we began organising a golf instruction book. Three years later, after many heavy discussions and lengthy taping sessions with Sandy (who put 100 plus per cent effort into this project), *Learning Golf: The Lyle Way* was completed.

What impresses me most about this book is the mental and physical completeness of the instructional message. You'll get the feeling that Sandy is standing next to you, encouraging you to "see" the shot, telling you how to set up to the ball, and spelling out what specific actions of the body you must make to swing the club correctly and hit anything from a straightforward chip to a super-powerful tee-shot. In the process, Sandy's knowledge of the swing, shotmaking expertise, and strategic sense, come through loud and clear.

By turning the complexities of the golf swing into easy-to-follow instruction, Sandy shows he is an excellent teacher, a communicator *par excellence*. And, if you are just half the student that he is a teacher, you will learn the game or play it better, by reading *Learning Golf: The Lyle Way*.

But don't let me sell you. Judge for yourself.

JOHN ANDRISANI
NEW YORK, March 1986.

INTRODUCTION

BY SANDY LYLE

I have never written an instructional golf book, so why should I now? Well, without sounding corny, golf has been good to me. It has given me personal fulfilment and allowed me to make friends with people all over the world. It has also provided me with material possessions that I would never have been able to afford otherwise. So, I think it is only fair for me to put something back into the game.

Nowadays, it is possible for some sports personalities to be so obsessed with money that they forget about the fans who make their dreams of fame and fortune come true and even believe they are bigger than the game they play. Not me. I refuse to walk away from my game, which is golf. I feel a commitment to show my appreciation and *Learning Golf: The Lyle Way* is my vehicle.

Actually, I have thought about this book for a long time. And although, in the past, I have stopped putting pen to paper on several occasions, I have never stopped writing this book in my head. You have to keep mental notes if you want to be any good at golf.

Being a perfectionist, I decided to wait until I was ready to devote sufficient time and effort to this work. I realised that dedicating myself wholeheartedly to this project was the only sure way to get my swing points and mental pictures across to you. Also, I wanted to be certain in my heart and mind that I could offer you crystal-clear instruction, based on a sure and simple method of swinging the club. That way, you could read the book, learn my keys, and then go right out on the course and apply them to your game.

Learning Golf: The Lyle Way is my book, and your master plan. By following it, and practising my tips, you'll drum technique into your muscle memory. Essentially, this process enables the basic swing motion to operate on automatic. In other words, you will be able to think less about how to hit the ball, and more about where to hit it.

The process of writing this book, seeing it come to life, parallels the evolvement of my career. Both took time and energy and would not have been realised without the help and support of others.

Developing a golfing mind and a shotmaking sense had a great deal to do with my father. For never-ending support, I lean on the shoulders of my mother Agnes, sisters Alison and Anne – the rest of the "A" team. And in case you don't know it, all golfers need support when the bounces fail to go in their favour.

As to *Learning Golf: The Lyle Way*, I owe a great deal of thanks to a couple of people. John Andrisani worked with me for many, many hours on the research and writing. A top-notch golfer, as well as an internationally known golf writer, his wisdom of the swing has been as precious as his penmanship.

I also owe thanks to illustrator Ken Lewis, who has done a wonderful job of interpreting my instructional message in pictures.

I'm proud of *Learning Golf: The Lyle Way*, a book that delves into the ins and outs of swing technique and shotmaking, so that beginners can enjoy the game from tee to green, and more experienced golfers can correct faults or learn new shots.

I hope that *Learning Golf: The Lyle Way* serves as your stepping-stone to golf. And I'd like to think that when you make your first par or eagle, that I had just a little something to do with it. Then, I'll be satisfied that I gave something substantial back to golf.

SANDY LYLE
WENTWORTH, SURREY, June 1986.

PART I

THE RIGHT APPROACH

CHAPTER I

THE GAME OF GOLF – THERE'S NO SPORT LIKE IT

To the casual onlooker, golf often seems a silly sport. Chances are, you picked up *Learning Golf: The Lyle Way* out of curiosity, so maybe you are just now outside the game, looking in. More than likely, then, you are baffled by stories of men and women waking at wee hours of the morning, to bang a wee ball into a wee hole. It's conceivable, too, that you have first-hand experiences, encounters with golfers that make you even more inquisitive. Strolling by the local links on a summer's evening, you spot players putting out on the 18th green as darkness falls. Or, in the cold of winter, you see golfers wearing mittens and woollen masks, trudging around the course, chasing balls. Or, you watch enthusiasts entertain themselves by starting a round in the pouring rain, and shake your head, wondering what is the game's luring attraction. Let me see if I can answer that question, since golf is my game. And I assure you, one day it will be yours – believe it or not.

The Challenge

Right now, swatting the ball looks simple, and the sport, silly. Just a matter of hitting the ball and chasing it. "How can that be fun?" you probably ask yourself. Once you pick up a club, however, and take a swing at a ball, you will start to appreciate the challenges golf can bring. I guarantee you will want to have another go, and another, and another, until you can send the ball sailing off into the sunset. In a short time, you'll know that golf is far from boring. You'll know it's exciting. And as soon as you learn that there is a knack to swinging, shotmaking and scoring, and start searching for it, you will want to play, play, and play. That's good. *Learning Golf: The Lyle Way* is your guidebook. It will assist you on your golfing journey, a journey that I hope lasts a lifetime. This book will put you on the right road and keep you there, providing you sacrifice some playing time for practice time.

The reason you will need to practise is that, unlike team sports, golf is an individual game. Success or failure is your responsibility alone. Your only true opponent: the golf course. If that sounds like a heavy weight to carry on your shoulders, you can lighten the load through preparation. I'll be honest with you, the only way you are going to come out a winner is by working on your game. If you spend a couple of hours each week grooving the fundamentals of grip, stance, posture, aim and alignment, you will build the foundation for a fine swing.

I know the word "practice" has the same sour ring as the word "homework", but, really, there are no short cuts to learning golf. Besides, if you follow a system and set goals for improvement, you'll be shooting low scores sooner than you think.

Golf is also a game that rewards success or failure immediately. Most of the time, that is. You see, Lady Luck enters the picture. Sometimes you will make a perfect swing, and a bad bounce will send the ball into trouble. Other times, the golfing gods will be on your side. I have won tournaments because of a lucky bounce and lost tournaments because of a bad bounce. The trouble is, most golfers forget about the good bounces, and get upset when things go the other way. It's a natural reaction. I used to get upset over bad breaks, until I faced one fact: golf is an unpredictable game. The key is to accept the bad with the good, and stay on an even keel mentally. Otherwise, you will get cross with yourself, and muck up your swing and score in the process.

The more you play golf, the more you will realise that every shot, every hole, and every round is a new experience. Scrutinising a lie so you can select the right club, setting up squarely to the ball so you can swing the club correctly, learning to save par from a spot of bother or to sink a long, curling putt, are skills you must learn, to make the experience of playing 18 holes fun. And you will. Sure, the game will drive you crazy, at first, but the more you play the more confident you will become. Once you get the hang of the swing, you'll be champing at the bit, anxious to go out and beat *that* course.

Golf is therapeutic, too. It will take you away from the hustle and bustle of the everyday world and allow you to discover aspects of your character you never knew existed. You might realise by playing matches that you are a more competitive person than you imagined. This discovery will give you more gusto in the real world.

On the other hand, you might find out that you are basically an impatient individual, and that this negative aspect of your personality is hindering your golf. You better believe, it will. Golf rewards patience and penalises impatience. Rushing your setup and swing is the fastest way to hit the ball wildly. By taking extra time on the course, you will gradually evolve into a more patient person, an asset that is bound to pay dividends in the everyday world. If you are reading me right, you can see that golf is not all about knocking a wee ball into a wee hole. It has many sides.

Golf is a game for the weak and the strong, the smart and the not-so-smart. The Davids of this world can play the game as proficiently as Goliaths. And although well-thought-out strategy is essential to low scoring, you don't have to be a genius to be a par shooter.

But the greatest thing about golf is that it is open to everyone, unlike years ago, when only the rich could participate in the pastime.

The Attraction

Forgive my sales-talk. If you really want to see if golf takes your fancy – if it's really true that the "bug" can bite – try hitting a few balls at your local driving range.

You will probably miss or top the first couple of shots, but once you hit the ball solidly, you will feel an exhilarating sensation that stretches from head to toe. My guess is, you will want to hit shot after shot until you are able to

retrieve that super sense of satisfaction. And just wait until you play a regulation course. That is when you will really get a taste for the game.

Teeing a ball up with friends on a fresh morning, hitting an iron shot off a manicured fairway, and putting the ball in the hole are all pleasurable experiences. But when you really smack a drive "on the screws", or sink a shot from off the green, you'll be jumping with joy.

Just being on the course, in the open air, away from the daily routine that sometimes bores all of us, makes for a delightful day. The whole time you are playing, you will be close to nature. And if the sun is shining and the sky is blue, while you walk in splendid countryside or near the seaside which borders a links course, you will be happy you started playing this heavenly game.

Nevertheless, be prepared: the game doesn't always go your way. Trouble lurks. Gorgeous trees can turn into gargoyles when you hit a wayward shot. This is when you have to use common sense and depend on self-control to see your way out of trouble. Trying to pull off a miracle shot, when the odds are against you, rarely pays off.

Golf will test you as you have never been tested before. The longer you play, however, the quicker you will learn one of golf's treasures: it teaches you to learn from your mistakes. Only by staying on your toes from tee to green will you shoot low scores.

Your Start

Golf is a sport for people of all ages, but the earlier you start the better, for the muscles and mind are more receptive in one's youth. All the same, whatever age you are when you decide to play, here's the best introduction: take a club and a few balls and practise on your own, letting your instincts run free, before you take formal lessons. This approach gives you a rough idea of what moves your body must make to swing the club. Then, a qualified professional can mould you according to your strengths and natural tendencies.

Your Goals

When you do make your golfing debut, don't expect to play par golf; no one burns up the course straight away. It takes all of us time to get into the "swing" of things. So, go unhurried.

There is an art to scoring, for golf is a game of finesse as well as fortitude. Developing a well-rounded short game, adopting a sound mental attitude and sticking to a sensible strategy, are as important as learning the big swing. This is why mastering the game takes years of hard work and dedication. However, you are as good as the next guy. Honestly, you can excel, as long as you learn the basics of the swing, practise, and stay physically and mentally fit through regular exercise and good eating habits.

Whether you are young or old when you start to play, avoid getting obsessed with score. Sure,
this sounds like a ridiculous statement to make, since shooting the lowest number on each hole is the name of the game. That's true, but you have to learn to crawl before you can walk. First, you must learn to swing. Second, you must learn to think. You won't learn these skills overnight, but when you do, the scores will come. Approaching the game a step at a time is one of the secrets to success.

I can't really guarantee that *Learning Golf: The Lyle Way* is going to turn you into a scratch player. But if you absorb my swing keys through purposeful practice, I think you will play a pretty decent game of golf. I admit, maybe you won't score like a pro every time you go around the course, but you will surprise yourself at least once on every hole. And that, my friends, is why we all play this game.

CHAPTER 2

MY PLAYING PHILOSOPHY – PATIENCE IS PARAMOUNT

I'm fortunate to have a father who is a golf professional. Ever since the age of four, when I first took an interest in golf, and throughout my career, he has passed on priceless knowledge of the swing and the game, all the time stressing the importance of learning the fundamentals. He taught me a simple technique and encouraged me to adopt a mental attitude that keys on patience and perseverance.

At the outset of my golfing days, Father was highly aware of one fact: "You can't put an old head on young shoulders." All the same, he stuck to a master plan. By planting seeds of wisdom in my youthful brain, he supplied me with vital basics, which I still fall back on today.

His straightforward swing tip, "Grip firmly, not grimly," still helps me swing smoothly in a pressure-packed moment of competition.

His equally straightforward strategic tip, "Keep your head," encourages me to pick my spirits up after a bad shot or hole, and to return the best score I can, no matter how gloomy the picture looks.

Already, it should be pretty easy to predict that "simplicity" is the one philosophy that governs my swing and strategic play. First, let me explain how I apply this philosophy to my technique.

Putting a 100 per cent perfect swing on the ball requires such a precise coordination of the mind and body that the motion cannot really be repeated exactly the same way every time.

This is why my father's early advice, to keep the swing as simple as possible, has always made such perfect sense to me. To accomplish this goal I spent many hours on the practice ground, grooving the fundamentals of grip, stance, posture, aim and alignment. Next, I worked on specific actions of the swing, such as the takeaway and my first move down, until, finally, I pieced together one free-flowing uninterrupted motion.

Today, I'm more convinced than ever that my method is the simplest around. I stand behind my swing for one key reason: it is easy to repeat under pressure. And the easier it is to repeat, the better chance I have of making square clubface-to-ball contact. My swing may not spell perfection, but since it runs on a special fuel called "fundamentalism", it's the next best thing.

I'm grateful to my father for his guidance; had he not encouraged me to stick to a short, sweet motion, I'd probably be testing out every in-vogue swing theory that is spouted weekly on the Tour. As it has turned out, maintaining a simple philosophy and having faith in my method allows me to say "No thank you" to these so-called "secrets" or "answers".

Learning Golf: The Lyle Way is my means of passing on to you my beliefs or philosophies for swinging the club and playing this great game. I am going to tell you everything I know about the game and take you down the road as far as I can. Then, you'll have to do a little self-searching, as I had to do once my father finished helping me construct a firm foundation, and cut the apron-strings, so to speak.

Don't get me wrong, I want you to base your swing on simplicity, as I do. I want you to be aware of all the advice I can give you, but I can only take you so far, for our human make-up differs so.

Sure, I can tell you to focus on one shot at a time, and to take bad shots in stride. But I can't teach you concentration or patience. I'm no genie who can give you confidence or courage or the will-to-win, either. No one can give you these fundamentals.

The longer you play, the more you'll see that golf's fundamentals cover a wide range of territory, and mean much more than gripping the club correctly or standing square to the target.

Fundamentalism is also about mental maturity – doing the right thing "upstairs". This means never giving up, getting on with the game through thick and thin. That, friends, is my simple strategic philosophy.

In my case, a will-to-win attitude is not about showing bravado. Had I adopted such a cavalier style, I surely would have won fewer tournaments around the world; a totally aggressive "Go for broke" strategy works for Seve Ballesteros, but not for me. I prefer to "grind" quietly, to pace myself, and to wait patiently for the door to open just a wee bit. Then I pounce.

My state of inner steeliness paved the way for me to win the 1985 British Open Championship – my first major – and climb back to the number one spot on the European Tour that same year. It was also key to my winning the Masters, at Augusta, in 1988. Obviously, then, this attitude is another of my fundamentals.

As to my future, I believe that if I stick to the fundamentals, on and off the course, winning will take care of itself. And this is the position that all of us want to attain, and maintain, whether we're playing for pleasure or money, or both.

What style you adopt in order to put yourself in a winning position is the question you must answer. Remember what I told you: I can only take you so far down the road.

CHAPTER 3

CHOOSING EQUIPMENT – YOU'LL PROFIT FROM A PROPER FIT

Choosing equipment is a lot like picking out a pair of slacks or a skirt. The look of the clothing must appeal to you and the fit must be perfect, before you make a purchase.

Golf clubs that are aesthetically pleasing induce confidence, but only if they comprise the correct grip size and type, lie, loft, length, clubface angle, shaft flex, and weight, will the fit be "on the money".

Even golfers who have the time and the inclination to keep up with the newest clubs on the market find it near impossible to do just that. Nowadays, it seems club design changes as quickly as fashion trends do. What's "in" one month is "out" the next.

Having been on the Mizuno staff for a number of years now, I am fairly close to club design, and often visit their factories to take a peek at what the clubmakers are up to.

I suppose this is an advantageous position to be in, yet, occasionally, I get so fed up with the fast changes in club design and the constant compulsion to switch to a more up-to-date set, that I throw in the towel. Taking a couple of days off, I visit antique shops or the homes of club collectors, searching for classic models of the 1950s. Sometimes, I'll find a real gem that suits my swing, and play with it for a few weeks. Inevitably, though, the club ends up in my closet, collecting dust. And I end up back at the Mizuno factory, to check out what I have missed.

Most pros are like me, a really fickle lot, who, jokingly, curse the manufacturers for designing so many top-quality clubs to choose from.

Where you're concerned, shopping for new clubs will not always be a matter of buying a stock set off the rack, for the pro has to take into account such factors as the size of your hands, your strength, height, the length of your arms and the natural way you set up to the ball and swing. In light of this intricate measuring, he might have to use modern tools to adjust the lies and lofts of a new set to suit you, or order custom-made clubs from the manufacturer.

Generally speaking, golfers with big hands prefer a slightly oversized grip; less powerful players need a whippy shafted club; tall golfers, who set their hands high at address, usually benefit by using clubs that are one to two degrees upright; and golfers with short arms should have their clubs lengthened.

In this modern age of advanced technology, there is another factor to consider when purchasing a new set of sticks: playability of the model.

Many of today's clubs are sole, heel and toe weighted. Sole-weighted sticks will help the novice and average golfer most, for this feature makes lofting the ball an easier task. The plus factor of sole weighting really shows up in utility woods, however, which are extra lofted clubs that slide through the grass like a sickle.

Heel and toe weighting increases the sweetspot of the clubface, making the club more forgiving on off-centre hits.

The influx of innovative design

is endless. Metal fairway woods, for example, also ideal for recovering from deep rough, are getting such rave reviews that some pros and low handicap players, who previously scorned non-traditional clubs, are testing these out and liking them. Metal drivers are a big hit, too.

Along with these clubs come new lines of lightweight clubs and 60-degree wedges. And to counterbalance the continuing flow of investment in cast-made irons (moulded), there remain the no-nonsense forged-iron blades, which have for so long appealed to better players.

I'm going to stop here, for the list of products goes on and on, and even I know that this is starting to sound like a promotional release.

Let me just add that new clubs are nice, and there are Rolls-Royces in every category, but unless they suit you, you might as well be swinging an old hickory-shafted model.

In view of this, here are some guidelines to help you make the right choice.

Grip Size

To promote feel and better control of the clubhead throughout the swing, a player with a small glove size should be fitted with thinner grips. Golfers with a large glove size will do better with handles that are built up slightly. Players with standard-size hands should stick to a stock grip.

The proper grip might sound like "small potatoes", unimportant, but it is a key feature of a golf club.

If the grip is too thick it prevents clubhead feel and stops the player's wrists from rolling correctly. This hinders the release of the hands in the hitting area, causing the clubface to open at impact, and the shot to slice.

Grips that are too thin encourage loose hand action, causing the clubface to close at impact. The result: a severe hook.

Grip Type

The two most common types of grip are rubber and leather. I prefer rubber as do most of the pros, although players such as Jack Nicklaus have always liked leather.

Lie

Lie is simply the angle the shaft makes with the ground, when the club is soled or sitting in the natural position. Tall players usually require an upright club, while shorter players, a flatter model. The biggest consideration in choosing a club with the correct lie is how high or low the player sets his hands at address.

Once a player takes his setup, the bottom, or sole of the club, must be almost flush to the ground. Actually, if a pound note can just be slipped under the toe end of the clubhead, the lie is correct. If the toe is sticking up considerably, the club is too upright. If the heel is off the ground, the club is too flat to suit the player's tendencies.

This feature of the club should not be taken lightly. If the lie is incorrect, the player will have directional problems because he will have to change his swing path and plane to suit the angle of the club.

STANDARD LIES
Woods and Irons

WOODS	LIE Degrees
1	55
2	55½
3	56
4	56½
5	57
6	57½
7	58

IRONS	LIE Degrees
1	55
2	56
3	57
4	58
5	59
6	60
7	61
8	62
9	63
Pitching wedge	63
Sand wedge	63

Loft

Loft is simply the degree of pitch built into the clubface. Depending on the degree of loft, the ball will fly high or low. If a player's tee-shots fly too low, he should be fitted with a club featuring increased loft. If the player hits the drive high and seeks a more piercing flight, he should order a less lofted club.

STANDARD LOFTS
Woods and Irons

WOODS	LOFTS Degrees
1	11
2	13
3	16
4	19
5	22
6	25
7	28

IRONS	LOFTS Degrees
1	17
2	20
3	24
4	28
5	32
6	36
7	40
8	44
9	48
Pitching wedge	52
Sand wedge	56

Length

Surprisingly, a player's height has little to do with being fitted for length. The distance of the player's hands from the ground is the key. Players with short arms usually need longer clubs, while players with long arms need shorter ones.

STANDARD LENGTHS	
Woods and Irons	
WOODS	**LENGTHS** Inches
1	43
2	42½
3	42
4	41½
5	41
6	40½
7	40

IRONS	LENGTHS Inches
1	39
2	38½
3	38
4	37½
5	37
6	36½
7	36
8	35½
9	35
Pitching wedge	35
Sand wedge	35

Clubface Angle

The player should be guided by his shot patterns when selecting a club with the correct clubface angle. If the golfer usually slices the ball off the tee, he should look for a driver with a drawface. If he hits hooks, he is better off playing a club with a square-to-open face.

Shaft Flex

I consider the shaft of the club its most important feature. The five basic shaft flexes are: extra stiff (X), stiff (S), medium (R), flexible (A) and ladies' (L). The markings on the bands of the shaft easily identify the type of flex.

On the whole, average golfers usually play better with medium shafts, while single-figure players prefer a stiff shaft.

The only type of golfer who can handle an X shaft and put the clubface on the ball squarely, is an extremely strong, flexible player with excellent timing. I have worked extra hard to build up my golf muscles and, therefore, generate such great clubhead speed that I need an X shaft for shotmaking control.

My caution to you is: don't fall into the trap of playing too stiff a flex for reasons of machismo. Select a shaft that suits your swing and strength.

The majority of lady golfers should play the standard L shaft, while stronger women players with good rhythm and tempo should try a men's medium flex.

I would like to see most young players using medium shafts, but, again, the shape of the shot is the truest guideline. If a player duck hooks the ball, chances are the club is too whippy. If he hits the ball low, doesn't feel a click at impact, and loses distance by pushing or slicing the shot, the shafts are probably too stiff.

Weight of the Club

Junior players who are just starting out and aren't fully grown should play with light clubs that feature a swingweight no higher than Do. Lighter clubs are easier to handle and will enable a youngster to groove the basic upward and downward motions of the swing.

Players who are a little older and stronger should be cautious not to pick a club that is either too heavy or too light. In a stronger player's hands, the light club has a tendency to be pulled off the correct swing path, so it is difficult to return it back to a square impact position. A heavy club can cause swing faults, too. Even if a player is strong, he should stick to a standard swingweight, somewhere in the D2–D3 range.

Golf Balls *Basic Types*

1 Two-piece construction: Surlyn cover, solid core.

Difficult to cut, rolls farther than other types, flies better in the wind, but ball's "hot" feel takes some getting used to when chipping.

The ideal ball for beginners.

2 Surlyn-wound: Surlyn cover, rubber interior.

Difficult to cut, doesn't roll as far as the two-piece ball, but promotes better feel.

The ball for Mr Average.

3 Synthetic balata: Soft cover, rubber interior.

Cuts easily, doesn't roll as far as the other two types of balls, but promotes excellent feel.

The scratch player's ball.

A Note to Parents

My father started me off, at the age of four, with a baffy, a lofted wooden club he cut down, so that its new lightness and length enabled me to swing easily and freely.

This club was an excellent learning tool. Practising with it helped me get a basic feel for the swing and taught me to manufacture shots by trying various setups and swing techniques.

Although I was too young to realise it at the time, this early education taught me imagination, or the ability to see several ways of recovering from one situation. Looking back, I'm sure this was my father's intention, part of his master plan. I'm convinced that without this one-club apprenticeship, I would never have developed the shotmaking arsenal I have in my bag today.

I do have one criticism of learning the game with only a wooden club: when you sole a wood, it sits on a shallow angle, making the club feel longer. Yes, even when it is cut down. Hence, the tendency is to swing the club more horizontally, or on a flatter plane – for the rest of your life. This is okay if you think your child is going to grow no taller than, say, 5' 9", because short-to-average-size players should swing flatter to coil and generate power.

In my case, however, I sprouted to 6' 1", and because I think taller players should adopt a more vertical swing, I would have been better off learning to play with a more upright club. In fact, from time to time, my swing gets flatter due to this early nurturing. Consequently, I have to spend hours on the practice tee, working out the problem.

There is no doubt in my mind that my sons will want to take up golf, either professionally or for pleasure. At least, I hope they do. This is why I have devised a training programme that I think suits all children. It's a scheme you might like to follow in teaching your son or daughter the game.

Stage 1

Start your child off with a cut-down nine iron, one of the shortest, most upright, and lofted clubs in the bag. Allow the child to tee up the ball until he can consistently hit shots airborne. Then, take away the tee and have him hit shots off the grass. Once he proves himself again, let him have a go with a shortened seven iron, then a five, then a three, and finally a fairway wood, all the time following the same incentive procedure.

Throughout this stage, the child is bound to experience more frustration than satisfaction. This, however, is only part of a golfer's maturing process, the key to developing patience, persistence, temperament – qualities he will need if he is to play the game to a decent standard, later on.

Nevertheless, your child will look to you for support, so don't pressure him by making him promises, such as offering him a new set of clubs if he learns rapidly. If his progress is slow, call it a day. Otherwise you are likely to discourage him for ever, and that's a big mistake.

Stage 2

Give the child a putter and let him practise on the green. Start him off with one-foot putts and work up to the longer stroke.

Following this simple system will give your child a feel for the stroke and allow him to build confidence along the way.

Stage 3

If your child is keen to continue playing after completing these two stages, you might want to invest in a junior set which comprises a three, five, seven, nine iron, three wood and putter. Starter sets are a step up from cut-down hand-me-downs, and designed especially for youngsters; they feature thinner grips, lighter clubheads, and flexible shafts.

Stage 4

If your son or daughter grows stronger and so does his interest in the game, teach him the basics of grip, stance, posture, aim, alignment, and swing technique. Then, let him hit shots at the driving range. Next, bring him to a par three course, where he can play with other beginners. This approach is better than sticking him on a course with adults; he'll be less self-conscious around novices and less likely to hold up play.

Stage 5

If his love for the sport continues, until he is about 10 years old, with no pushing on your part, it will be helpful for him to take a few lessons, to see if he is moving in the right direction. If he is, it might be time to invest in a full set of used clubs. I don't think you should invest in a new set until your child is fully grown, unless, of course, you can afford it.

Whenever you decide to buy your child – or yourself – a complete set of clubs, make sure you know what you are shopping for.

The Rules of Golf only permit you to carry 14 clubs, so choose a combination that best suits your game. With the array of new models flooding the market place, the standard set, comprising a driver, three and four woods, 2–9 irons, pitching wedge, sand iron and putter, is becoming a rarer sight.

If you are a beginner, you might want to exchange a two and three iron for a couple of super-lofted woods. You top-notch golfers might want to swap a four wood for a one iron or a third wedge. The choice is yours. What's crucial is taking the time to put together "your" set. Don't let anyone kid you, clubs can make the man.

PART 2

FUNDAMENTALISM

CHAPTER 4

THE GRIP – HOLD ON TO THE CLUB CORRECTLY AND YOU'LL HOLD ON TO A SOUND SWING

In an ideal swing, the club moves in harmony with the body. Since the hands are the only parts of your body that are directly connected to the club, the way you grip the club is crucial.

To give yourself the best possible chance of swinging the club back along the proper path, up to a secure position at the top, and down, so you strike the ball squarely and solidly, you must hold the club in the right manner. Make no bones about it, the grip is the "engine room" of your swing.

Basically, there are three different ways of holding the club: with a full-finger, overlapping or interlocking grip. The choice you make is a personal one, but you should take into consideration the size and strength of your hands.

Throughout my golfing career, I've actually played with all three grips, and although each is distinctive, there remain a few characteristics that hold true to form. And it's these principles that you must adhere to, no matter which grip you choose to play with.

Four Foolproof Grip Checks

Fingers are feelers

The first of these principles is the way you wrap your hands, or "feelers", around the grip end of the golf club. The grip should lie across the base of your fingers and partially in the palm of your left hand, while resting predominantly in the fingers of your right hand.

Palms Parallel

Getting the hands to work as a team is my goal every time I grip the club. To accomplish this basic I put my hands on the club as if I were slapping both of my palms together. This way, my hands are "square" to my target.

In other words, after gripping, if I were to open my hands, extending my fingers and letting go of the club, my palms would be "square", or at right angles to the target line – the imaginary path that runs from the ball to the target.

It's easy for your hands to slip out of this parallel position during a round, so get into the habit of

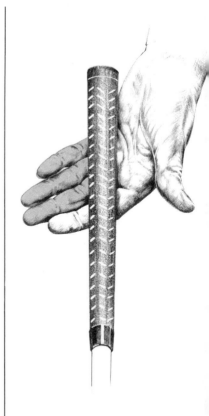

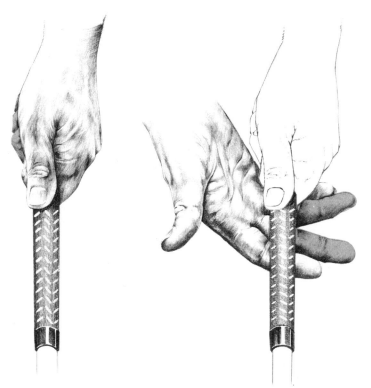

Whether you choose to follow in my footsteps and play with an overlapping grip, or feel more comfortable with either a full-finger or interlocking hold, is not so essential as sticking to a set of principles that govern the way you wrap your fingers around the club and, ultimately, the manner in which you swing.

The grip end of the club should lie across the base of your fingers and partially in the palm of your left hand, while resting predominantly in the fingers of your right hand.

Both of your thumbs should rest on the sides of the grip, not point straight down the shaft.

As a general rule, you should grip a wee bit more firmly with the last three fingers of your left hand and with the middle two of your right.

checking your palms each time you sole the clubhead. This palms-parallel hold might feel un-comfortable in the beginning, but if you stick with it, you will not be sorry.

No varying the Vs

Another checkpoint that I use to confirm that my hands are gripping the club properly is the position of two Vs, formed by the thumb and forefinger of each hand.

Once you take your setup (standing so your body line is square, or parallel to the target line, spreading your feet approximately shoulder-width apart, bending slightly from your knees and waist, and placing the clubface squarely behind the ball), look down and verify that the Vs are in the "neutral" position – pointing midway between your chin and right shoulder. If they are not, I guarantee you will be in big trouble, unless you are capable of working miracles.

Holding the club with a "weak" hold – one in which the Vs point up at your chin – usually causes the clubface to shut or point towards the ground in the backswing, and open in the downswing. This shut-to-open swing is likely to produce a slice, a shot that flies drastically to your right.

Ironically, many pros, including myself, play with a weak grip. The only reason I can control the ball, while using such a weak left-hand hold, is that I have grooved a sound swing, by hitting thousands of practice balls, and have been blessed with big hands, to boot.

Those of you who are just starting out should stick to a neutral grip. However, as you progress as a player and your hands get stronger, you might like to weaken your hold, ever so slightly.

Once you juggle your fingers into position and set the clubface squarely behind the ball, look down at your hands. The V formed by the thumb and forefinger of your right hand should point midway between your chin and right shoulder, while two-and-a-half knuckles of your left hand should be visible.

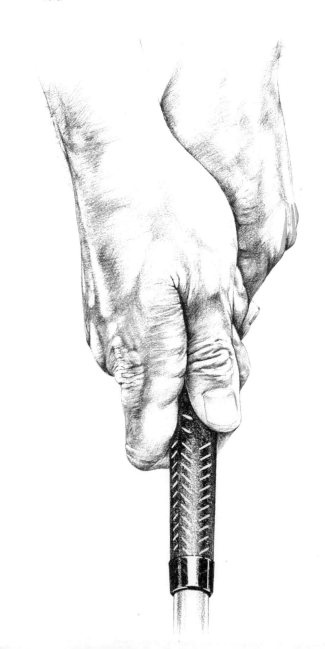

If the Vs point to your right shoulder at address, the grip is "strong" and you will probably swing the club around your back in the takeaway, up on too flat a plane, or angle, and over the top of the ball in the downswing. At the moment of impact, the clubface points left, instead of at the target. The result: a hook.

My advice, then: stay away from adopting a strong grip. And, if you already hold the club in this fashion – switch. If you need some further assurance that this is not the grip for you, look around. You'll rarely see a top PGA Tour player or amateur using a strong hold.

Proper pressure

Squeezing the grip with just the right amount of pressure is the fourth principle you must adhere to.

As a general rule, you should grip a little more firmly with the last three fingers of your left hand, and with the middle two fingers of your right. To make certain that you are neither "choking" the club, or holding it too loosely, during practice or a friendly game, ask one of your parents or a playing partner to pull the club from your grasp. If both of you feel just a slight resistance as the club slides through your fingers, your grip pressure is perfect. This means you are holding the club lightly enough to feel the clubhead and firmly enough to withstand the forces of impact. In my father's words, you are gripping "firmly, not grimly".

During a serious competition when you are not allowed to seek the advice of an opponent, look for shotmaking signs to detect a faulty grip. Weak shots can often be traced to a strangle-hold grip and inaccurate hits to a gentle hold.

My First Hold on the Game

When I first started playing golf, my father's major concern was that I follow the principles I have just spelled out, but because my hands were small and weak, he encouraged me to use the full-finger or "baseball grip" as the Americans call it.

I would never dream of using this grip today, for two reasons: 1. My hands are larger due to natural growth, and stronger due to regular exercise, and 2. I think holding the club in this fashion makes me too much of a "handsy" player, and that is against the laws of the swing as I see them.

The hands should serve more as "connectors" than "controllers". Although you certainly key on your hands, this all goes on unconsciously, unless, of course, you're stripping apart your swing during practice – trying to learn, and groove, a particular pulling-down motion. Once this hand motion is incorporated into your swing, through practice, you should get the sense that you are hitting the ball "through" your hands, not "with" them.

Reading this, you may be wondering why my father instructed me to use the full-finger grip. The answer is a simple one,

and, again, it comes back to strength.

As a boy, I was not flexible enough to coil my body, nor powerful enough to generate clubhead speed by driving my legs and whipping my arms in the hitting area. Therefore, I had to depend on my hands. The full-finger hold worked best, because all my fingers gripped the club.

Grip Types

Before describing the three types of grips, I would like you to set up to the ball and grip the club in your left hand only, as follows.

Wrap your first four fingers around the butt end of the club and then lower the thumb, so it rests to the right of centre, on the grip. Check your V and be sure that when you look down you can only see two and a half knuckles. This position of the left hand remains constant, no matter which grip you choose to play with.

Right. Now you are ready to set your right hand on the club, holding the grip with your fingers and placing your right thumb on the left centre of the rubber or leather end.

Full Finger

This type of grip requires you to turn all the fingers of your right hand under the grip, with the pad of the right hand covering your left thumb. That's it. All you need do, now, is check that the palms are parallel to each other and that the Vs of each hand point midway between your chin and right shoulder.

Overlapping

The overlapping or Vardon grip, popularised by Harry Vardon, one of golf's greats (who grew up on the island of Jersey), is the grip I started using in my junior days, and despite a brief spell five years ago, when I experimented with the interlocking hold, it is the one I intend to continue playing with.

Now that I've mentioned this experimental period, let me relay to you a funny story – one that will shed some light on my thinking process, and show you the importance of mind over matter.

Prior to the 1984 Lancôme Trophy at St Nom La Bretesche, I was hooking tee-shots, so decided to switch from an overlapping to interlocking grip.

Before actually making the change, I brainwashed myself into believing that the new grip would cure my hooking problem, by stopping my right hand from controlling the downswing.

My caddy was shocked, unable to conceive of how I could dream of making such a change so close to the start of this prestigious event.

Like all struggling golfers, I guess I needed "something" to believe in. The interlocking grip was my ray of hope, although I didn't think of it this way at the time.

The gimmick worked. I won the tournament in a playoff with Seve Ballesteros, and played quite well for several months afterwards.

Then, out of the blue, I began hooking the ball more violently than ever. When I discovered the "real" fault – an especially flat backswing – the truth hit me, straight away. During that brief spell of sensational ball striking, I had tricked myself into believing that the interlocking grip de-activates the right hand slightly. In my heart, I knew this wasn't true at all; this grip (like the full-finger hold) encourages the hands to work more actively. But the switch boosted my confidence, and somehow allowed me to swing on a more upright plane. This new attitude, and not my new grip, is what cured the problem – for a while anyhow.

Crazy? Not really. Just a case of turning the tables by "believing" differently.

Okay, enough stories. Let's get back to the Vardon grip.

This grip is used by the majority of European and American Tour professionals and although I will not argue with success, I only recommend this type of hold to the player who has long fingers, strong hands, or constantly fights the hook.

The Vardon grip tames your right hand, so that it is less apt to overpower your left and shut the clubface at impact.

To take the Vardon grip, either lay the little finger of your right hand over the top of your left fore-finger or rest it in between that finger and the middle digit of your left hand. Then wrap the rest of your fingers around the club, so everything falls into position.

Interlocking

To take the interlocking grip, work the little finger of your right hand in between the first and middle finger of your left hand. Then, juggle the remaining fingers into position, around the grip, and check your Vs.

A number of players such as Jack Nicklaus claim this type of hold allows the hands to work as a team. In theory, this once made sense to me. But the more I played with this grip, the more I could feel my hands fighting each other for control. I think the reason for this power struggle is that my hands are big, unlike Nicklaus, who has tiny mitts.

Nevertheless, I did discover through trial and error that the interlocking grip allows me to work my right hand independently of the left, a basic action that could come in handy for playing a few lofted shots around the greens, such as the lofted sand shot or pitch from deep rough. Since I am for ever looking to learn new shots, I will fool around with this grip during my short game practice, and if my own theory is right, I may be a two-grip player, one of these days.

I hope I haven't made the task of selecting a grip sound complicated. It's not. Just remember, that no matter which grip you choose, stick to the principles. Otherwise, you are cheating yourself. And no professional or amateur can afford such luxuries.

CHAPTER 5

STANCE AND POSTURE – GOOD BALANCE IS A BONUS

Errant shots are frequently traced to a discombobulated setup. The reason is, most golfers try to play by instinct, instead of being more scientific about the way they position themselves to the ball.

Even I know how easy it is to slip into a faulty address, one that feels right and gives me the sense of power, but one that is wrong and usually causes me to hit the ball weakly and way off line.

Strange as this may sound, some days I might hit every ball solidly and straight, too, from an incorrect setup position. This is because, for some inexplicable reason, I manage to make the perfect compensation of the body and club. More often than not, however, if I'm playing the ball in the wrong spot, setting up with too wide or narrow a stance, stooping over or standing up too tall, or I'm over- or under-extending my arms, my shots fly inaccurately.

This is why I go through a checklist every single time I address the ball, and if I stick to it, I know I will cut down the odds of

making a silly mistake. And that, my friends, is one of the secrets of playing to your potential. So, take it from me, go through a regimented rehearsal at address, and you will be on the road to real fine form.

Address Rehearsals

BALL POSITION: I play almost all my shots a few inches to the right of my left heel. I'll only move the ball forward or back from this spot if I am hitting a speciality shot.

Many teachers and Tour pros play the driver, fairway woods, and long irons off the left heel, then move the ball back a hair each time they switch to a more lofted club. Not me; I believe in simplicity. I feel the least number of changes you make to your setup, the more you'll stay on top of your game. Nevertheless, ball position is somewhat of a personal choice, so don't be afraid to experiment.

CAUTIONS: 1. Playing the ball too far forward causes you to hit either a high or "thin" shot and, 2.

Playing the ball too far back in your stance causes you to hit either a low or "fat" shot.

STANCE: When I am hitting a tee shot, the width of my stance (measured from the inside of one heel to the other) is about 14 inches. I narrow the stance infinitesimally to play fairway woods, long and medium irons. My stance shrinks to about a foot's width, when playing full short irons or hitting putts. It is slightly narrower than that when I hit chips, short pitches or bunker shots.

CAUTIONS: 1. An extra-wide stance causes you to swing on an exaggerated flat plane. Common shot: hook. 2. An extra-narrow stance causes you to swing the club on too steep an angle. Common shot: slice.

POSTURE: This, I think, is the most crucial aspect of your setup, so pay close attention. No two golf professionals swing exactly the same, but when each takes his address position, their postures

Because the setup predetermines the swing motion, you must stand comfortably and correctly to the ball.

Flexing your knees, bending slightly from the waist, and allowing your arms to extend in a relaxed fashion, puts you in position to swing the club on the proper path and plane.

pretty much match each other. The posture of almost any pro is somewhere between a soldier's attention and at-ease position, neither too tense nor too relaxed. This is the one I strive for, and so should you.

The player who is unorthodox over the ball must have superb flexibility and feel for the clubhead. He must be able to manipulate his body and the club, so that by the time he reaches impact, he looks like every other top golfer in the world. But players such as Japanese star, Isao Aoki, who gets away with stooping over at address, are rare breeds. So, don't get any wild ideas.

To play every club, I stand erect, with my chin up and a couple of inches away from my chest. I also focus both eyes on the back of the ball.

To help me set my hands free of my body, I bend slightly at the waist.

Pushing my hips back creates a slight curvature at the back of my spine and makes my bum stick out, so that I am in a semi-sitting position.

Cracking my knees enables me to distribute my weight equally, between the ball and heel of each foot.

CAUTIONS: 1. Stooping over disrupts balance, a key to accuracy; 2. Resting your chin on your chest restricts your shoulder turn, so your shots lose power; 3. Looking at the top of the ball causes topped shots; 4. Positioning your hands too close to your body encourages you to swing the club on an out-to-in path, causing you to hit a slice, and 5. Putting too much weight on your toes or heels, when you are faced with a level lie, discourages leverage, which I call the disguised key to picking up those extra yards.

ARM EXTENSION: Regarding the setup, the question I am most often asked is: "How far should I stand away from the ball?" I never answer in terms of feet and inches, otherwise the player will start thinking too much about this measurement. My answer: "Far enough away from the ball for the arms to extend in a relaxed fashion and for the sole of the clubhead to sit almost flush on the ground."

CAUTIONS: 1. Overextension causes tension and prevents the proper rotation of your wrists, and 2. Underextension causes you to break your wrists too early in the swing.

Since these are heavy prices to pay for minor mistakes, it is essential for you to know "your" distance.

CHAPTER 6

AIM AND ALIGNMENT – SEE THE SHOT IN YOUR MIND AND SET UP SQUARE TO YOUR TARGET

I consider myself a fast player, sticking to a steady stride in between shots. However, once I begin my preswing routine, I take time to see the shot come to life in my mind. Then, I juggle my body and the club into position. In most cases, this means to set my knees, hips and shoulders parallel to the target line, with the clubface aiming dead at the target.

It took me years to realise that preparing to swing the club and strike the ball squarely and smartly requires as much mental as physical energy.

Visualising a positive result, or "seeing the shot", sends a message to your subconscious mind. By tracing an imaginary line from the ball to the target and actually seeing the shot happen, you tell your subconscious exactly where and how you want to hit the shot. Once the message is programmed into your mind, the body will find a way to follow instructions, providing you set up squarely to your target.

The intent of alignment is to set your body in a workable position, one that allows you to swing the club along the path needed to produce a particular shot. If your setup is finely tuned, this will happen almost naturally, without any manipulation of the club with your hands.

One little mistake, however, and all is lost, for the swing demands such a precise coordination of the mind and body that even a small error is a big one. For example, if you want to hit the ball on a direct line, from point A to point B, and you aim either your body, or the club, too far left or right of the target, you will almost always fail to achieve your goal, no matter how smooth your swing.

To help you learn the basics of setting up, I will run through my preswing routine for driving the ball:

STEP ONE: I start my routine the moment I tee up. Standing behind the ball, I look at the shape of the hole, the hazards, check the wind conditions, and if I can see the flag, or know the pin placement, I focus on a section of the fairway that I can hit an attacking approach from. Let's assume, for the purposes of getting the elements of my preswing procedure across, that I have determined that I want to hit a drive dead down the middle of a tree-lined fairway.

STEP TWO: Still looking down the hole, from behind the ball, with the driver in my hands, I stare at my target and see the shot fly solidly off the clubface, splitting the fairway in two.

STEP THREE: I usually take a couple of practice swings, to rehearse the motion. However, it depends on my mood. Often, I have played 18 holes without taking a practice swing from behind the ball.

STEP FOUR: I walk up to the ball from the side, nearly always taking a practice swing, to rid my body of any tension. Then, I put my right foot in the basic position for a driver stance, and place the club squarely behind the ball. All the

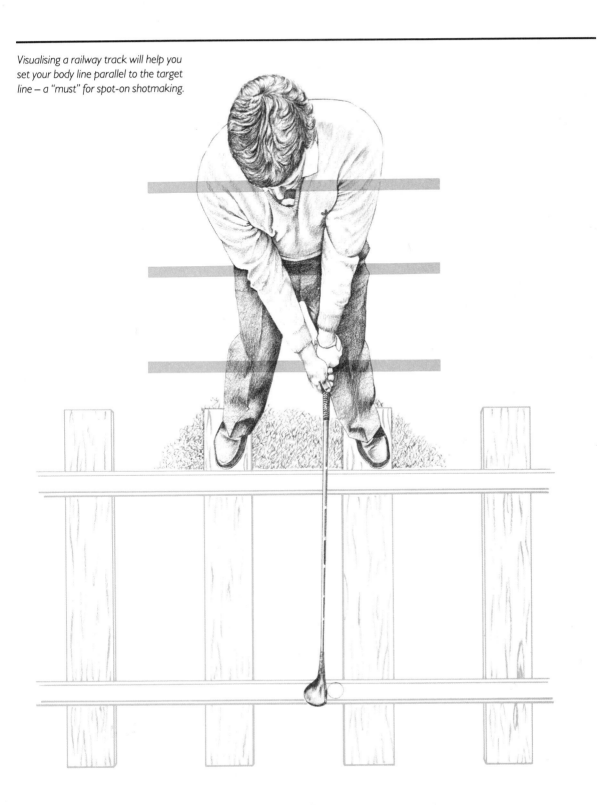

Visualising a railway track will help you set your body line parallel to the target line – a "must" for spot-on shotmaking.

time I am doing this, I am fooling with my hands, working them into place.

STEP FIVE: I step fully into the shot, jockeying my feet further into their final positions, so I am playing the ball a few inches to the right of my left heel, and so the toe of my left foot is fanned out slightly more than the right.

STEP SIX: I make certain that my feet, hips, and shoulders are parallel to the target line, confirm that the clubface is aiming dead at the target, and the Vs of both hands are in the correct positions.

STEP SEVEN: I set myself further into position, checking my posture and making sure my left arm and the clubshaft form a straight line.

STEP EIGHT: After looking back and forth from the ball to the target, two or three times, I hover the sole of the club slightly above the ground, pause to encourage a slow takeaway, then swing the club.

Note: Before you swing, you might want to "waggle" the clubhead, moving it backward a couple of inches along the target line, and forward again, returning it square to the ball. Doing this will prevent you from "freezing up".

SPOT-ON-TARGETING

Many Tour players, such as Jack Nicklaus and Greg Norman, the Australian, aim at an interim target, a few yards in front of them, instead of at the one in the distance, because they claim it is simpler and serves as a safeguard against misaligning. This target can be a leaf, a divot – it doesn't really matter as long as it sits along the line they intend to hit the ball.

Players who incorporate this system into their preswing routines say it gives them an added sense of security. Each one feels sure he is setting up with his body and the blade square to the target.

Personally, I feel I am missing the entire picture if I line up this way. I can only feel comfortable if I focus on a landing spot in the fairway, when I am driving the ball, or on the flag or a section of the green, if I am hitting an approach. As I have pointed out already, I truly believe this is the only sure way to send a positive signal to your brain. Nonetheless, if you feel out of sorts setting up to a distant target, give spot-alignment a try. It just might suit you and help you raise your game.

PART 3

MY TECHNIQUE – AND YOURS

CHAPTER 7

THE LONG SWING – A WALTZ IS BETTER THAN A QUICKSTEP

In my mind, the number one reason why the high handicapper has trouble sweeping the ball off turf or a tee (with a wood or a long iron) is because he sets up as if he were playing a short club. Standing closer to the ball, putting more weight on his left foot, crouching a wee bit more than normal, and setting his hands close to his body, low, and ahead of the ball, all cause him to swing a long club like a short club – on a steep plane. I'm afraid this is like mixing oil and water, for the lower numbered clubs are longer and less upright than the shorter ones and should be swung on a shallower angle of ascent and descent. However, you don't have to worry about achieving this shallow swing plane if you set up correctly and make a strong turn away from the ball.

Yes, it comes back to preswing preparation. Position your body properly at address and the club's lie will dictate your plane of swing. The flatter club will swing on a flatter plane – just what the doctor prescribed for hitting a solid sweeping shot.

Now that I've sold you on the benefits of a sound setup, let's take a look at the keys you must learn. To play any long club, you must:

1. Play the ball a few inches behind your left heel; 2. Set your body and feet parallel to the target line, and point your knees in towards each other for added stability; 3. Toe out both feet, your left more than your right; 4. Take a comfortable and correct posture by bending only slightly from your knees and waist; 5. Put 50 per cent of your weight between the ball and heel of each foot; 6. Allow your left arm and the clubshaft to form a straight line, while your right arm bends slightly; 7. Aim the clubface perpendicular to the target (setting your hands in line with the ball will encourage spot-on aiming) and 8. Keep your head behind the ball, with your eyes looking at its back dimples. I agree, this is a long list, but the more you practise this setup position, the sooner you'll groove it.

Before I review the keys for making a full, free-flowing long swing, there are a few concepts you must understand:

The target line is an imaginary line that runs from the ball to the target.

Everything to the left of this line – on your side of the fence – is called "inside", or inside the target line.

The territory to the right of the target line is called "outside".

Now, the swing.

The start, or "takeaway", is one of the most important stages of the swing. If the initial move you make away from the ball is incorrect, there is little chance that you will be able to get the swing back on track and achieve your ultimate goal – the one all golfers strive for – square clubface-to-ball contact. The only way to bail out a bad start is to try to reroute the club back along the proper path and plane by jerking it. But do that and you'll destroy your natural tempo and rhythm, and at best hit a shot that finishes several yards off line.

Even an experienced player, like me, who has the ability to sense an early error, can rarely correct it in midstream and hit the shot as planned. The entire swing takes less than two seconds, so our reflexes can't react quickly enough to redirect a faulty start.

If you watch the game's best players in action, you'll notice that their takeaway actions are deliberate. Making a slow, smooth start is the only way to ensure a strong coiling action of the body and a full weight shift to the right side in the backswing – two keys to powerful and accurate strikes. In my father's words, "A waltz is better than a quickstep." He believes what I believe: take it slow at the start and you'll establish good overall tempo, a must for putting the club squarely on the ball. Make a fast takeaway and you'll be talking to yourself after a few holes.

The player with a fast takeaway may get away with such a faulty move if he's grooved the action by hitting thousands of practice shots and if his timing is tops. Sooner or later, however, his swing will go to pieces, due to either a pressure situation or the law of averages.

The way to repeat a timed takeaway is to put yourself in the mood to swing the club slowly. Picture the word "tempo" inscribed on the top of the club's wooden head or on the face of a long iron. Run a mental movie that shows you taking the club away smoothly. Or just remind yourself that you're out on the course for enjoyment.

But I'm getting ahead of myself. Let's examine my first move, called a one-piece takeaway, a common trait among top-notch players, and a term you will hear many times throughout your golfing life.

Basically, a one-piece takeaway means swinging your left arm and the clubshaft back together, or in one piece. Unless a pro is a "handsy" player, like Seve Ballesteros, he'll make this move. However, he might not trigger the takeaway in the same way his playing partner does.

One pro may start the swing by pushing off with the ball of his left foot. Another will rotate his left knee or hip to the right, or away from the ball. Another will swing his left shoulder towards his chin, while still others will key on

---

Once I confirm that my setup is sound and that I am comfortable and confident over the ball, I glance back and forth, from the ball to the target. Then, just before I start my swing, I lift the club up slightly, so the sole hovers a wee bit above the grass.

Hovering the club behind the ball is unorthodox, but this adjustment encourages me to extend the club back further along the target line – a move that promotes an extra-wide arc. You might want to try copying this feature of my setup if you repeatedly lift the club straight up in the takeaway.

Hovering the clubhead encourages a one-piece takeaway.

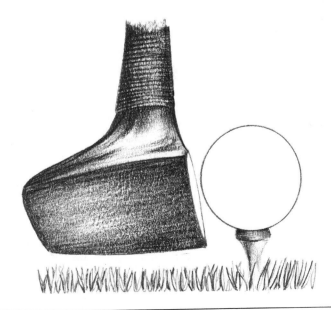

pushing the club back with the left hand or pulling it away with the right.

I'm proud to say I'm different. Believing in unity, I synchronise the movements of my left shoulder, arm, the clubshaft, my left hip and knee, away from the ball. As long as I keep my left arm straight, my wrists locked and turn my shoulders during the initial start, the club will swing back along the target line, then to the inside.

One mistake the high handicapper makes in the takeaway is to pull the club away inside the target line. Consequently, he loses power because he fails to turn, and loses accuracy because he pulls the club so far behind his back that he is unable to return the clubface squarely to the ball at impact. Once again: if you set up to the ball correctly, keep your wrists firm and turn your shoulders, you will "automatically" swing the club to the inside in the takeaway. There is no need for any conscious manipulation of the club with your hands.

I don't want my hands to do anything else but hold on to the club. If I'm making a proper takeaway action, I feel as if I'm swinging the club "through" my hands, not "with" them. Maybe this sounds like a matter of swing semantics now, but after you have played the game for a while, you'll see it is a matter of swing "fact".

Day in and day out, I'm asked the same questions: How long should the clubhead swing back relatively low to the ground in the takeaway? And why?

You should swing the clubhead back until you feel weight shift to the inside of your right foot. For all you mathematicians, this is "about" 18 inches. However, you will do better to go by feel, rather than fact.

Why should you swing the club back low to the ground initially? So you can return the club low to the ground in the hitting area and sweep the ball from a tee, or the turf at the exact moment of impact. If you pick the club up quickly in the takeaway, you pull it straight back down. And that's the last move you want to make when swinging a long club.

Once the majority of your weight shifts to your right foot, your right leg should brace to prevent any swaying. As soon as this bracing occurs, a message is sent to your brain: "Okay, now it's time to swing the club up."

At this point, I feel my left heel wants to be pulled off the ground, but I leave it planted because I am striving for a "short" long swing. The only time I allow my heel to lift is when I'm looking to hit the big ball off the tee.

You might do better to "let" your left heel lift, if you feel that your turning action is restricted. If this is the case, freeing your foot will serve as an aid in swinging the club upward. However, don't ever consciously lift your left heel in the backswing. Wait until you feel it "must" be lifted, otherwise you'll run into all sorts of swing problems. Often, the high handicapper who lifts his heel sways off the ball, moves his weight to the outside of his right foot, and finds it extremely difficult to time the downswing.

If I were to stop and take inventory of my swing, once my hands reach waist level, the reading would be: 1. Head still; 2. Left kneecap even with the ball; 3. Left shoulder nearly under my chin; 4. Upper body coiling; 5. Right leg braced with approximately 70 per cent of my weight on the inside of my right foot (when I reach the top, about 80 per cent of my weight is on my right foot) and 6. The back of my left hand is virtually parallel to the target line.

If I continue on course (swinging on the path and plane I grooved in practice), I will maintain the straight line relationship formed by the back of my left hand and the back of my left forearm, throughout the backswing. In other words, there is no concavity or convexity at the back of my left wrist. More important, though, is that my hips and shoulders are continuing to turn away from the ball. Essentially, it's these two synchronised coiling actions that will swing the club up.

There is no sudden jerk with either of my hands to move the club upward. Again, it is my ongoing turning action that is sending the club upward. Both my sides are coiling, not just one. This is why I think that the neverending question, "Is golf a left-sided or right-sided game?", is gibberish. Make no mistake: golf is a two-sided game.

Once I reach my destination, at the top of the swing, which for me is the three-quarter point with the longer clubs, I am fully coiled and the back of my left hand is parallel to the target line.

Here, I have a momentary feeling of waiting for my lower body to start triggering the downswing motion. But this is just a feeling, for I know that some part of my lower body is always moving.

So, I don't actually pause, as the novice may think when looking at me change directions. If I were to pause, that would mean all movement would stop and then have to start again. But you can't do that and swing the club fluidly. Some part of your body always has to be moving for the swing to be a swing – one continuous uninterrupted motion.

I like to think of my swing as a range of tones. If my tempo is "on song", the speed of my swing builds up steadily, just as the pitch of a singer's voice gets higher and higher as he goes from *do*, to *re*, to *me*, to *fa*, to *soh*, to *la*, to *te*, to *do*.

I prefer this image to saying "one", as the club swings from the address to the top of the swing, and "two", as the club swings from the top to impact. To me this gimmick, which is most commonly taught, tampers with tempo. First of all, it sets up a pause at the top, which is against the laws of the swing. Second, it makes no sense, for the swing should not be thought of as two halves, and certainly not two equal halves. It should take you approximately one and a half seconds to swing the club from the address position to the top. And a mere fifth of a second to return the club from the

1 *Left arm and the clubshaft line up. Square setup.*

2 *Initial backswing turning action.*

3 *Left knee behind the ball. Controlled three-quarter backswing.*

4 *Initial downswing uncoiling action.*

5 *Left arm and the clubshaft return to an in-line position. Head still behind.*

6 *Left arm folds slightly at the elbow. Right arm is fully extended. Head still behind.*

7 *Belly button faces left of the target. Weight on the outside of left foot. Hands high.*

top, to impact. So, don't fall into the trap of thinking that "one" equals "two". The swing beat is not split up into two equal parts of approximately one second each, it quickens as the club comes closer to hitting the ball.

I depend on my left hip and knee to start the downswing. Rotating these two body parts (in unison) back to a square position (as they were at address), and then to my left, enables me to shift my weight back to my left foot, and makes room for my arms, hands and the club to swing down to, and through, the ball. Yes, my arms and hands are "swung" through, as is the club, which returns first to the target line, then moves to the inside after the hit. When my goal is to achieve a sweeping action, I don't make any conscious effort to pull the club through.

To hit through the ball and to achieve the sweep with the longer clubs, you must stay down longer through impact, by transferring your weight to the outside of your left foot and by firing your right knee towards the target.

Some of you players might be wondering why I have not mentioned the "release", a word that frequently comes up during talks about technique. It is certainly not because I want this book to read like a mystery novel, but rather because I don't think the release is that crucial. Before you go jumping off your seat, allow me to explain.

The typical high handicapper has heard the word "release", and has a rough idea that this means to let his right hand roll back on top of his left, through impact. The trouble is, he tries to make this happen once he reaches the top, by rolling his right forearm over and flicking his right wrist and hand. Forget the release, for it happens after the hit, not before. More than that, it is a "result" or a response to other correct swing moves. It is not a move you consciously make with your hands, as so many novices think.

If your backswing position and downswing hip drive are sound, the hands will respond, allowing you to put the club squarely on the ball. And that is what matters most. Trying to make a conscious effort to work your hands destroys everything you worked for. Letting the ball get in the way of a good swing, and not hitting "at" it, is the answer.

The follow-through and the finish of the swing are more reactions to the backswing than premeditated acts. But you should still check two key positions, to see if you're swinging at the highest efficiency level.

In the follow-through (when your hands reach waist level), the back of your right hand should be parallel to the target line.

When you complete the finish, almost all your weight should be transferred to the outside of your left foot and all but the toes of your right foot should be off the ground. As a final check, be sure that your belly button faces a hair left of your target. This position proves you have cleared your left side and made a free and fluid swing. If you need any further confirmation, look at the ball flying down the middle of the fairway.

Power

It's in a golfer's nature to want to boom the ball out of sight. Take my advice: stick to the straight shot until you get a good sense of just what makes your technique tick.

I admit, the player who drives the ball far and straight down the fairway has a distinct advantage over the shorter hitter. The "bunter" has to play a longer club into the green, which is more difficult to hit and control than a shorter, more lofted iron.

Nonetheless, the power hitter is not necessarily the better golfer. As I eventually discovered, there is a lot more to the game than sheer length. Realising this, I usually swing at 85–90 per cent of maximum speed.

There will, however, come a time when you will have to incorporate a couple of power keys into your swing. You'll need added length to carry fairway bunkers or large expanses of rough when hitting a tee shot.

There's no secret to hitting the long ball, but, honestly, no short cuts either. All of the solid ball strikers I know use a swing that is founded on fundamentals and follow a simple formula to generate power.

When I want to "let out the shaft", I "think" power straight away and visualise the ball zooming down the fairway. Then, setting the clubface squarely to the target, I focus on the back of the ball – my contact point.

My setup is a little different from normal; I put myself in a power position by playing the ball off my left instep, put 60 per cent of my weight on my right foot, and get a real sense of my left shoulder being higher than my right, which allows me to feel the oneness of my left arm and the clubshaft.

Putting a little more weight on my right side discourages me from reverse pivoting. That's when you leave your weight on your left side in the backswing, and on your right in the downswing.

Playing the ball forward encourages me to stay behind the ball in the downswing – a big key to achieving big power.

My overall goal is to make a strong turning action. I know that if I coil like a spring in the backswing, and unwind coming down, I will generate high clubhead speed and really compress the ball with the face of the club at impact.

My takeaway has to be extra slow to promote a longer extension action of the club along the target line, and a bigger body turn.

By the time I complete my backswing, I know if I'm on track, when pressure builds in my right foot and leg. Swivelling my head to my right slightly strengthens the coiling action I am trying to achieve.

Continuing back, I allow my left heel to rise off the ground. Freeing the foot sets off a positive chain reaction that helps me get

*Hit against a left-side wall and you'll
wallop the ball.*

my hands in a higher position at the top of the swing. In turn, this move triggers a bigger arc.

At the completion of the backswing, the clubshaft is parallel to the flight line. Allowing your left arm to bend slightly will make it easier to drop the club into this position. Nevertheless, be careful. If you let your arm bend too severely, you run the danger of pointing the club off target. If the clubshaft points right of your target, you will swing from inside to outside the target line. The result: a slice. If the clubshaft points left of the target, you will probably deliver the club to the ball from outside to inside the line. The result: a pull.

In the downswing, I set up a leverage action by replanting my left heel and allowing pressure to build under my left foot and up my left leg. I have a sense of holding back because I don't want to let my upper body get out ahead of my lower body.

Now that I have this firm left-side wall to hit against, I am confident that I can make a fearless swing. Keeping my head behind the ball and allowing my right side to drive more upward than forward, I whip my arms through and make super-solid contact on the upswing.

TEMPO TIP: FOR SLOWING DOWN

Quick tempo can cause you to shut the clubface at impact. The result: a severe hook. To tame your tempo, practise hitting six iron shots as far as you normally hit an eight iron.

Working on this drill will encourage you to swing with the same basic tempo with every club in the bag, instead of swinging a lot harder as the clubs get longer.

After just a short session on the practice tee, you will put your swing tempo right. And your shots will fly straight, not crooked.

TEMPO TIP: FOR SPEEDING UP

When you "think out" a swing, it lacks sufficient speed. As a result, the club fails to return to a square position at impact. It is open, and an open face usually means a slice.

To speed up your overall tempo, tee six balls up in a row, a few inches apart. Then, walk up to each ball, settle quickly into your setup and swing the driver without thinking. Now your swing will flow, not freeze up. And your tee-shots will fly towards, not away from the target.

BEAT THE "FLATS" WITH A BRICK WALL IMAGE

Many golfers exaggerate the movement of the club inside the target line in the backswing. An overly flat swing can cause a number of problems. Among these, a faulty turning action and fast tempo — two errors that cause the ball to fly off line.

Depending on how fast or slowly you rotate your hips (from this faulty backswing position) in the downswing, the shape of shot you will hit can range from a vicious hook to a vicious slice.

In trying to hit the ball hard, I run into this problem occasionally. And so will you.

To help you swing the club to the inside, but not on too flat a plane, imagine that there is a brick wall about two feet behind your back. This is a trick my father taught me, and one that works. This image will encourage you to swing your shoulders, arms and hands more up than around yourself, so you set the club securely at the top.

One caution: make sure you don't make the mistake of imagining that your back is right up against the wall. If you do, you will probably "pick" the club straight up, on too steep a plane, and that is just as harmful as a flat backswing action.

CHAPTER 8

THE SHORT SWING – KEEP IT COMPACT FOR CRISP CONTACT

I compare playing the long clubs to hitting a high-speed tennis serve, and playing the short clubs to hitting a soft lob. The former spells power, the latter, precision.

Unlike the longer clubs, the shorter ones feature a high degree of loft. So each club, from the seven iron to the sand wedge, will accommodate a steep angle of descent and give you the spin you need to land the ball softly on the green, from the long or short grass.

You'll usually be hitting the short irons to the green from about 90–130 yards out in the fairway, so they are the "scoring" clubs. To make them work, you have to make a shorter, more compact backswing, and use a descending blow to send the ball flying high into the sky.

I think the best avenue to becoming a proficient short-iron player is to set up so the swing takes care of itself. This might sound like too simple a solution, in the light of all the complex chat you have heard in the past regard-ing specialised short-iron technique. But, since I truly believe that the setup predetermines the swing motion, here goes:

Although I still play the ball a few inches behind my left heel, my address for the short irons varies slightly from the one I use to play the less lofted clubs. The reasons are simple: I want to key on different parts of my body and put a different swing on the ball; again, more steep than shallow. To programme steepness into my swing, I:

1. Stand closer to the ball; 2. Take a narrow open stance, but keep my knees, hips and shoulders parallel to the target line. (My left foot is set back a couple of inches from an imaginary line that runs across my toes and that is usually parallel to the target line. I fan my right foot out only slightly, but I believe you will further encourage a steep plane by keeping the front of your right foot perpendicular to the target line); 3. Put 60 per cent of my weight on my left foot, and 4. Set my hands a hair ahead of the ball.

In the takeaway, I turn my hips and shoulders more vertically than horizontally (as I would if I were playing a longer club). As always, the clubhead starts out along the target line, but now, due to this upright turning action, it swings only a smidgen inside.

When my hands reach chest height, the steep plane and swinging weight of the clubhead causes my right wrist to cock. From here, I swing the club up with a slow tempo, to a point somewhere between the half and three-quarter position. Throughout the action, head rotation and body stretch are minimal, unlike the long swing, when I'm looking to accomplish a strong turn of my hips, shoulders, and upper torso. Although weight shifts to my right foot, I'm cautious not to get over zealous by allowing my left kneecap to turn inward, behind the ball. My knee-cap stays in line, or even a couple of inches ahead of the ball. This somewhat restricted knee action contrasts sharply with the lower body action I use for a long swing windup. However, it prevents lateral sway and allows me to set

Key on driving the back of your left hand at the target (in the downswing), and the clubface will return to a square impact position, every time.

MY TECHNIQUE – AND YOURS

the club in a secure position at the top.

Once I initiate the downward motion by rotating my left hip and knee back towards the target, and transferring weight to my left foot, I only key on keeping my head behind the ball. This might sound silly, but not if you remind yourself that the downswing only takes one fifth of a second. Focus on one key and you will be in control; on more than one, and you will be confused. Stay behind the ball and the rest of the action will take care of itself. First your arms swing down, then your hands, then the club.

In the hitting area, the back of my left hand leads the way. If all goes right, it will face the target at impact. My head is still behind the ball during the hit. If I were to allow my head to move ahead of the ball, my shoulders would point well left of the target at impact (instead of being parallel to the target line), causing the clubface to close and the shot to fly left.

When you stay behind the ball, you put yourself in position to hit the ball while the clubhead is moving slightly downward – before it reaches the bottom of its arc, shallows out, and starts upward. Contacting the ball while the clubhead is moving downward helps you achieve backspin, which in turn offsets any sidespin that might cause the ball to curve off line.

How do you know when you have stayed behind the ball and made the proper downswing? Let me put it this way: you won't have to ask a friend or look at yourself swinging on video to find out.

You'll "feel" the proper action. Pressure builds under the ball of your left foot as you stay behind the ball and wait for the club to swing down. The leverage action that is created allows your arms to swing the club down on a steep angle, so the clubface strikes the back of the ball and the club's leading edge cuts the turf. Once it does, your right side and head release fully, and the club swings through, then up.

1 Slightly open stance.

2 Steep angle of ascent.

3 Braced right leg.

4 Initial uncoiling action and downswing weight shift to left foot.

5 *Left-side hip clearance. Left arm and clubshaft return to an in-line position at impact.*

6 *Right-side release. Club in classic toe-up position. Back of the right hand is parallel to the target line.*

7 *Full finish: right foot straight up and down, hands high, weight on outside of the left foot.*

Putting "Stopspin" on the Ball: An art worth learning

No doubt, you have watched a tournament professional back the ball up on the green with a short iron, and wondered how on earth he could hit such a super shot. Trust me; getting the ball to spin back might look like a Herculean task, but it's not. I know it appears to be a trick shot that only a pro can conjure up, but you can get the ball to do more than a dance on the putting surface. You can get the ball to stop, almost dead. Putting this soft-cut shot in your bag will allow you to attack the stick, with no fear of the ball backing up into a bunker.

By now, it shouldn't surprise you that the setup is crucial, so let's take a look at just how you should address the ball and swing the club in order to produce "stopspin".

For starters, play the ball midway in your stance, point your feet and body well left of the target line (open), and set the clubface squarely to your final target. Now, put as much as 70 per cent of your weight on your left foot.

Playing the ball back and putting a high percentage of your weight on your left foot, shortens the takeaway and steepens the backswing.

The open alignment (aiming left) further encourages a steep swing and also allows you to move the club away from your body (outside the target line) on the way up, and towards your body (across the target line) on the way down.

The resulting shot will fly from left to right, so make sure you allow for the curve at address. In addition, cutting across the ball cuts out power, so make the correct compensation when choosing a club. If, for example, the distance calls for a nine iron, play an eight.

Since this speciality shot requires only a slight turning action, I want you to leave most of your weight on your left foot as you swing the club up to the half-way point, using minimal wrist cock. "Feel" the club move to the outside.

In the downswing, you should feel your arms, hands, and the club swinging from outside to inside, an action that will allow the clubface to cut across the ball, rather drastically, at impact.

To hit the shot properly, you don't want to take as deep a divot, so you'll have to come out of your knee flex sooner and strive for an upward follow-through and finish.

The shot you hit will fly high and sit down softly, the moment it hits the smooth surface of the putting green.

PART 4

THE SHORT GAME

CHAPTER 9

PITCHING – SELECT A SPOT ON THE GREEN AND HIT TO IT

Golfers who can pitch the ball close enough to the hole for an easy one-putt conversion, can never be counted out of a match.

Hundreds of times, throughout my pro and amateur careers, I thought I had a hole "in the bag" until an opponent hit a super pitch over a trap, to a tight pin placement, or played a perfectly judged pitch-and-run.

The pitch stroke is shorter than the one you use to play full short-iron shots. Just how short the swing is depends on how far you are from the spot you select for landing the ball and the type of shot you want to hit – a high or low pitch.

The players whose pitching games impress me most have to be Seve Ballesteros and Tom Watson. Neither of these two professionals were just born gifted. They have both worked extra hard, and still do, to engineer ways of playing the pitching wedge from all sorts of situations.

Pitching used to be the weak link in my game, but over the last few years I have developed quite a shotmaking repertoire, from the basic stroke to more imaginative play. Mind you, I do not consider myself a magician. Nonetheless, by experimenting with several ball, clubface, and setup positions, and swing techniques, I have learned how to invent shots, a knack that enables me to salvage par from some pretty sticky spots.

Any pitching expert knows this talent requires more "finesse" than "force". And each specialist credits his skills to solid practice.

If the words "pitching practice" put you to sleep, you will have to do what I did: wake up. A couple of hours of practice, per week, is the only way you are going to evolve into a pitching master, unless you are so rich that you can play the game every day. Sorry folks, but those are the facts you must face. And the sooner you face them, the better.

When you are prepared to devote some time to working on your pitching game, be sure to structure your sessions, so you groove at least one key every day. Throw-

ing down a dozen balls and pitching them haphazardly from one side of your garden to the other is really just going through the motions. If you're concentrating on your stroke, that's another matter, but most amateurs who practise like this get bored quickly. Therefore, they tend to rush each pitch or start fooling around, hitting ridiculous shots. If you fall into this category, remember this: practice is practice is practice. There is no other way.

If you hit pitch shots in your own garden, or on the practice ground, you are better off playing three balls, and having a specific purpose in mind for each shot you play.

Try to loft the first ball just over a rope, stretched across the grass, 15 feet in front of you. Pitch the second ball just over another rope, 30 feet away. Both these exercises will teach you touch, the ability to match the length and speed of swing to distance.

Next, the real test: the final ball. Put a bushel basket in between the ropes and pretend that you have to hole the pitch to win a match or the Club Championship. It might take you a while to fly one in the basket, but when you do, you will know you are getting closer to becoming a wedge wizard. More than that, all the time you are practising you'll be having fun. And when you do get out on the course, you'll find it easier to evaluate a lie, pick a landing spot, and pitch the ball "dead" to the hole.

I really believe that any golfer can learn the multifaceted art of wedge wizardry and put a multiple of shots in his bag. The secret is perfecting the basic pitch and pitch-and-run, first, for almost all other greenside shots are offshoots of these two techniques.

To teach you these shots, I am going to walk you through two situations that you'll surely face on the links, giving you two simple solutions.

Basic Pitch

YOUR SITUATION: The ball is sitting up in light rough, 15 yards from a pin that is cut close behind a yawning greenside bunker.

YOUR SHOT: BASIC PITCH. This is a lofted shot that will carry the hazard and stop quickly on the green. To help you pull off this shot, programme a positive result into your preswing routine: see the ball land and stop next to the flag.

YOUR SWING: Instinct will tell you to play this shot like an ordinary short iron; however, the technique required is very different indeed.

Your goal is height. But, to accomplish lofted ball flight from this particular lie, going down after the ball and taking a divot is not the answer.

In contrast to the full short-iron shot from the fairway (when you hit down to impart backspin on the ball), the basic pitch from this common type of lie calls for you to hit the ball on the upswing with only a little leverage action from your lower body.

Just because I say to lessen the leverage action, I do not want you to think I mean to leave your legs out of this shot. On the contrary: your knees must be active. Simply speaking, you will feel less pressure on the ball of your left foot at impact because you will be swinging the clubhead through the ball softly, instead of into the back of the ball with a firm blow.

In doing so, you will throw the blade under the ball, lifting it cleanly from the grass, so it floats over the trap and lands softly.

Once again, the setup is critical; it predetermines the motion. So, take your time to settle into position and get on with the job as follows:

Address

Play the ball slightly forward of your normal position for the wedge.

Set up open to the target line, with a narrow stance, and put a wee bit more weight on your right foot.

To pop the ball in the air with a pitching wedge, you must work your right knee towards the target and allow your right foot to rise in the downswing.

Grip a touch more lightly to enable your wrists to work freely, and choke down on the handle for added control.

Aim the clubface squarely at your target, but lay the blade back to help you loft the ball.

Bend at the knees, more than usual, to encourage good footwork and make certain your left arm and the clubshaft form a straight line.

Backswing

As you sweep the club back only a hair inside the target line, get a sense of your knees rotating and the rest of your weight rolling from the inside of your left foot to the inside of your right. Allowing your left heel to rise enables you to swing your arms freely and your hands back almost to shoulder height, in a relaxed fashion.

Keeping your head relatively still throughout the motion prevents you from swaying.

Downswing

Maintaining the steady head position, roll your weight back to your left foot.

To help you catch the ball on the upswing with a clean sweeping action, work your right knee towards your target, quicken your arm speed and try to put your left hand in your left pocket.

Of course, you cannot possibly put your left hand in your pocket, but this mental key will encourage you to swing "through", not "to", the ball. With all this help, the ball can do little else but float like a butterfly, and land as quietly as one, too.

To play a longer and higher pitch, work your right shoulder under your chin and turn your right hand under your left, through impact. Getting the feeling that you are picking the ball off the ground with your right hand and tossing it (underhand) in the air will help you execute the high pitch. The higher you want to throw the ball, the higher your right arm moves upward. The same is true with the swing; the higher the pitch, the fuller the finish.

Pitch-and-Run

YOUR SITUATION: Your ball is sitting in the middle of the fairway, 10 yards off the edge of the green and 25 yards from a pin cut on the top level of a two-tier green. No hazards guard the front of the putting surface. The lie is tight, the green firm, and a strong wind is at your back.

YOUR SHOT: PITCH-AND-RUN: This is a low shot that lands well short of the pin and runs up.

YOUR SWING: Playing down wind, an extra-high pitch will not hold the green. The sensible strategy is to play the percentage shot – the Scottish pitch-and-run.

To execute this shot properly you have to pick a spot to land the ball, either in front of the green, or on the lower level of the putting surface, so that it bounces and then rolls the rest of the way.

Hitting a perfectly paced pitch-and-run shot takes practice. However, you can expedite the learning process by keeping your right foot planted and your hands ahead of the clubhead through impact.

This decision depends on the speed of the green, its firmness and the strength of the wind. If, for example, the green was extremely fast running and the following wind was, say, 25 m.p.h., you would have to land the ball short of the green.

It is called the "Scot Shot" for good reason. On a Scottish links, the turf is tight and the greens are extremely quick. The putting surfaces are also undulated, so even a lofted pitch can come down and carom off a bank, into a bunker. Hence, if you face such a puzzling lie, the pitch-and-run is a handy tool.

The key is to make a short compact swing, leaving the wrists almost entirely out of the shot. This technique enables you to nip the ball, so it flies on a low trajectory, lands, bounces, and scoots up to the hole.

Address

With the ball played opposite the central point in your stance, put the majority of your weight on your left foot.

Take a slightly open stance, but keep your body virtually parallel to the target line.

Choke down and grip more firmly to discourage exaggerated wrist action.

Set the blade squarely behind the ball, dead in line with your target.

Standing up to the ball with quite an erect posture encourages you to work the club with your arms, enabling you to nip the ball

neatly from the tight turf.

Setting up with your hands ahead of the ball will decrease the effective loft of the club, a key to hitting the run-up.

Backswing

Keeping your feet planted and weight left, swing the club back along the target line and up to waist height, with little or no wrist cock.

Since this is strictly a "feel" shot, there is no need to build up torque by turning your body. So, unless the shot is an extra-long one, the left shoulder should never turn fully under your chin.

Move your knees ever so slightly and key on making a free-flowing swing with your arms.

Downswing

The key to the downward motion is keeping your hands ahead of the clubhead – a must for pinching the ball with the pitching wedge.

To further ensure a low-ball flight, you'll need to strive for a low follow-through. That's no problem, so long as you keep your knees "quiet", right foot planted, and slow up your overall swing tempo.

CHAPTER 10

CHIPPING – LET YOUR WRISTS KEEP A LOW PROFILE

Whenever the ball sits in the fringe, a few feet off the edge of the green, and approximately 15–50 feet from the pin, I expect to chip the ball close. And so should you.

Strokes add up quickly; if you can save one or two from around the greens, by chipping like a pro, you can stay ahead of the game.

The reason the chipping game of the average club golfer suffers is due largely to one mistake: flicking his wrists, in an attempt to help the ball up. Although I can understand his logic, it's the wrong approach. This fault can lead to a number of bad shots, namely a top, caused by the clubhead's leading edge contacting the top of the ball. Topping the ball will send it rolling quickly, well past the pin, and probably through the green. One more shot that results from overactive wrists is the fat. The clubhead stabs the ground behind the ball. Thus, the shot comes up short of the hole.

Another common error shared by the majority of high handicappers is lack of concentration. They take the chip for granted, simply because it is such a short shot. This is no excuse. Hitting thousands of chips during practice and play has taught me to bear down, no matter how short the shot. To be an expert chipper you must always give full attention to the shot. If your mind wanders, so will the shot.

I find that if I fail to concentrate intently, I end up leaving myself testing putts for par. And when you have to face a lot of these putts in the course of a round, your stroke eventually succumbs to pressure.

This is why you must take care to: 1. Evaluate the lie and the distance to the flag; 2. Pick a spot to land the ball; 3. Select the proper club; 4. See the shot come to life in your mind; 5. Settle into a sound setup; 6. Rehearse the actual stroke, by taking one or more practice swings; and, 7. Allow the arms to control the basic actions of the stroke.

This probably sounds like a long list, but sticking to a preswing routine is the only way you are going to play to your potential. If you want to walk off the eighteenth green proud of your play, then it is going to take some work out on the course. If you are out there merely for the exercise, that's a different story, although, quite candidly, I have never believed that anyone plays the game solely for that purpose. Chances are you play golf to shoot the best score you can, so give it your all.

Selecting the right club, more than any other factor, makes chipping a complex art. Some top golfers believe in hitting one club, usually a sand wedge, for almost every chip they face.

I admit, I hit a lot of high, low, short, and long chips with my sand iron, but I am never dead set on sticking to this club. I always wonder if another club will service me better. Most of the time this "other" club is an eight iron, but sometimes it's as low as a four. The fringes on most courses are cut low, so my club selection depends more on the distance to the flag, and strangely enough the mood I'm in. One day I might face a short chip, and want to put a gentle stroke on the ball with, say, a seven iron. Another day, I might face a long chip, and because I am in an aggressive mood, I select a sand wedge and put a firm stroke on the ball.

Don't misunderstand me, I have nothing against a player using a favourite club. In fact, I think it is best for you to play a club you are confident with. Just be careful not to slip into the trap of choosing an "old faithful" to hit every chip.

Let's say for argument's sake that you face a 20-foot downhill chip and the seven iron is your favourite club. Well, unless you are a shotmaking genius, you will run the ball several yards past the hole. The seven iron doesn't feature enough loft for you to land the ball softly, when rolling it down a severe slope. In this case, you would be better playing either a nine iron, pitching wedge, or sand iron.

The only true way to become a specialist at selecting the right club is to practise. Hitting chip shots with several clubs, from, say, the four iron to the sand wedge, will tell you exactly what kinds of shots you can play with each. That way, when circumstances arise on the course, you will "know" what club to play, because you have already practised the right kind of shot.

Looking back and forth at a spot on which I want to land the ball is what helps me match a technique to the club I choose, out on the course. This spot will be closer or further away from the hole, de-pending on the loft of the club. Basically, the more lofted the club, the closer to the flag you will need to land the ball.

I am quick at making decisions around the green, due to the eye-to-hand coordination I have developed in practice. Playing all types of chip shots has allowed me to store up quite a memory-bank of shots. Nevertheless, even though I am probably more of an expert than you at reading a situation and seeing the shot, I still have conditioned myself to go over a preswing checklist. Adhering to a disciplined routine is the only way that you can confirm that your choice of club, and the shot you want to play, are right. If there is only a touch of doubt in my mind as I take my address, I step away and re-evaluate the variables that come into play. Being quick off the mark will only mess up your scores. So, again, don't rush. Be ready.

Taking your practice swing seriously is also especially crucial when you're playing a chip. It would be nonsensical for me to try to recommend to you a set number of practice swings. Everyone is different, but the points I am making are: avoid nervous swats and wait until you are ready before you play.

You can see that there are no quick routes to becoming a chipping ace. As with most things in life, experience helps. All the same, if you groove the basic stroke that follows, you'll feel more chipper the next time you face a chip shot from the fringe!

Setting up so your hands, arms, and shoulders form a triangle, and reconstructing this shape in the downswing, keeps your chip stroke sharp.

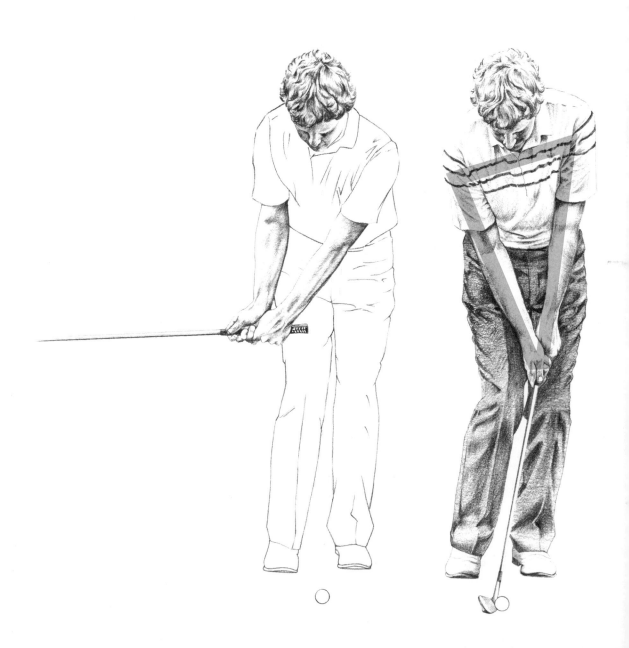

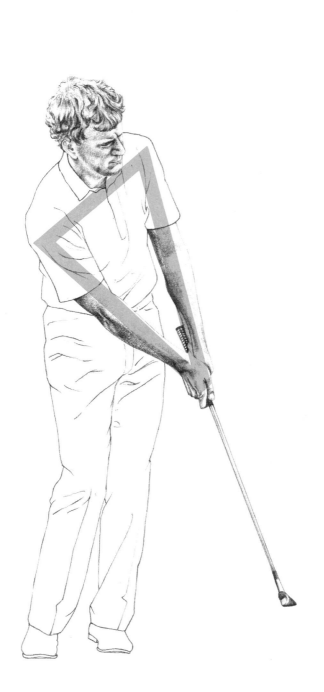

Chip Stroke

YOUR SITUATION: The ball is sitting up in the short fringe, five feet off the edge of a green that is relatively level. The distance to the flag is 35 feet.

YOUR SHOT: BASIC CHIP. The ball will carry the fringe, land on the green, and roll most of the way to the hole.

YOUR TECHNIQUE: I will be honest, you can play this shot with a variety of clubs. I'd probably play a sand wedge, and even though I use the same basic chipping stroke to play almost all my shots from the apron, this is not the club for you, or the percentage shot.

Now, the last thing I want you to think is that I am talking down to you. I am not. When I started playing golf, I wouldn't dream of chipping with a sand wedge. Only through years of experience have I learned to use this club effectively from greenside lies. Without sounding as if I am sitting on a pedestal, this club requires perfection to pull off the shot. Anything short of that, and you are in trouble. Listen to this story and you'll see what I mean.

I almost blew the 1985 Open Championship on the 72nd hole by trying to hit an extra-delicate chip with my sand wedge. My second shot finished pin high, 35 feet from the flag. Then I tried to loft the ball to the crest of a little hillock on the green, so it would trickle down to the hole. Unfortunately, I landed the ball only inches short of the spot I wanted it to hit, and it came rolling back almost to its original position. Fortunately, my father's advice to "Keep your head" came to mind, and I managed to two putt and win. However, now maybe you believe me when I say the sand wedge can be a suspect club to play, even for a pro like me.

I suggest you play an eight iron, a club that is lofted enough to give you confidence, and so forgiving that if the shot doesn't come off exactly as planned, the ball will still finish close enough to the hole for you to make the putt.

Address

Take a narrow open stance and with the ball played almost midway between both feet, keep your weight on your left side and hands ahead of the ball.

Opening your stance gives you a clear picture of the target, while setting your hips and shoulders square to the line enables you to swing the club on an inside-square-inside swing path.

Grip normally, choke down, and be certain that your left arm and clubshaft form a straight line. To help alleviate tension, allow your right arm to bend at the elbow.

Imagining that a line drawn across your shoulders and down both arms and hands forms a triangle will give you a sense of these body parts working as a team. The fewer moving parts to the swing when playing a chip shot, the better. If you can reduce the number of moving parts there is less to go wrong, and a more consistent stroke is the result. So, feel the triangle to get a sense of "oneness".

Backswing

Leaving your weight on your left foot, keeping your head relatively still, and your lower body "quiet", swing the club back low to the ground. Then, allow your right wrist to cock and your right elbow to tuck in close to your body.

If you have had former instruction or read other books, my suggestion to cock the right wrist probably shocks you. Before you misinterpret what I am telling you, and run out to the practice green, trying to hit chips by allowing your right wrist to "snap" in the backswing, let me explain. I want you to use your right wrist, but it still should keep a low profile, bending only enough to promote feel and prevent you from getting too robotistic. Breaking the right wrist drastically will only lead to flicking the wrist at impact. That spells disaster, just as trying to keep the wrists stiff causes tension and loss of feel. So, allow the right wrist to give a little, not a lot, and encourage the arms to swing by keeping the lower body quiet, as you swing the club up to thigh height.

Making too long a backswing is a common fault of the high handicap player. The funny thing is, he senses this and compensates by decelerating the clubhead into the ball. The result: a mishit.

The fact is, the clubhead must be accelerated through the ball, and to do that the backswing must not be too long. By the same token, the backswing mustn't be too short, either. Otherwise, you will stab at the ball and, once again, hit a chip that you are not happy with. Consequently, you must find the right compromise. The best way to do that is to drop a few balls on the practice green, and chip away.

FOOTNOTE: The only time you should use a stiff-wristed stroke is when you face an extremely long chip, usually uphill, and decide to run the ball up to the hole with a long iron.

Downswing

Directional control is all-important here. To achieve this, move the back of your left hand towards the target and straighten your right arm. These two actions will enable you to re-establish the triangle you formed at address, and promote a nice smooth swinging action of the arms.

To help you accelerate the clubhead and make clean contact at impact, work the right knee inward.

CHAPTER 11

BUNKER PLAY – SPLASHING THE SAND IS THE SECRET OF SUCCESS

The bunker shot scares most golfers, but don't let it scare you. It is really simple to recover from sand, whether the ball is sitting up or down.

If it makes you feel any better, bunker shots baffled me once, too. Instead of setting up carefully, swinging smoothly and letting the club do the work, I usually made one of two mistakes: 1. I tried to pick the ball cleanly and hit a top or, 2. Swung violently, sinking the blade too deeply into the sand, and hit a fat shot.

The setup and swing for playing any kind of bunker shot is unique. The Rules of Golf prohibit grounding a club in a hazard, so having to hover the blade above the sand takes some getting used to.

Fortunately, a sand wedge has 56 degrees of loft and a thick flange, with bounce, a special feature that enables the clubhead to skid through the sand and splash the ball out safely – if you let it.

The proper club won't solve all your problems, however. To tackle troublesome bunker lies, you must learn to control the backward and forward movements of the club almost solely with your arms and hands, while working your wrists actively. The right mental attitude is equally important; your frame of mind can make the difference between leaving the ball in the bunker or blasting it out. So be confident, and visualise a positive result.

Most of the time you will run into two types of level lies: ball sitting atop the sand or ball buried. The distance to the hole will vary, and you will have either a little or a lot of green to work with.

Because of these contrasting situations, the swing techniques differ, so let's take a close look at the mechanics involved.

Short Sand Shot: Clean lie, little green to work with

This is the most common sand shot you will face, and before you go rushing into a swing, remind yourself of your objective: you want to loft the ball high, so it carries the lip and lands softly on the green. Sending this message to your brain allows you to "picture" this very result. It also encourages you mentally to rehearse the right technique, which is a relatively steep back and through swing.

With the ball played forward in your stance, opposite your left heel, aim your body left of the target line. Setting up open to the target line creates a V-shaped arc, which causes the ball to rise quickly and stop quickly.

To help you feel the sand's texture and gauge how easily the blade will slide through it, wiggle your feet into the sand slightly. Now, put about 60 per cent of your lower body weight on your right foot, to give you the sense of staying "behind" the ball.

Grip normally, with your hands slightly behind the ball, but juggle the blade until the face looks skyward. This adjustment increases the effective loft of the club, another aid in achieving height.

Break your wrists early in the takeaway and swing the club back

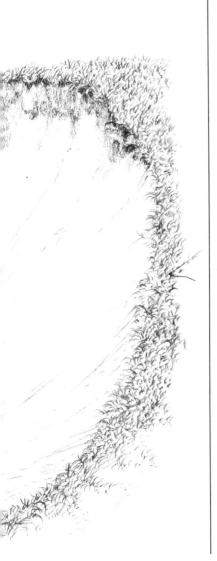

along your body line. Stop when your hands reach chest height.

By swinging the club outside the target line, you set up an out-to-in swing, one that produces a shot that starts out where your body is aimed, and cuts back towards the flag.

In the downswing, you must maintain the loft of the club by slapping the sand with its flange, about an inch and a half behind the ball. This is the surest way to prevent disaster occurring, by virtue of your right hand crossing over your left in the hitting area.

Slapping the sand allows your right hand automatically to turn "under", not "over" your left, through impact, and the blade to slide through the sand as if it were moving through butter.

Long Sand Shot: Clean lie, lot of green to work with

To play this shot, you must use a technique that varies slightly from the one I have just described.

You want to play the ball opposite the middle of your feet.

You still should set up open, but avoid aiming so far left, because your objective is to create a flat-bottomed arc for lower trajectory and added distance. Spreading your feet a couple of inches wider than shoulder width and setting your hands in line with the ball will promote a shallower, more U-shaped swing arc.

To help visualise this shallow arc, remember what it's like to splash a friend with water at the beach or in a swimming pool, when he's not very close to you. In order to splash him, the base of your hand must contact the water on a shallow angle of descent, then skim along its surface. Apply this same principle when playing the long sand shot, and you'll like the result.

The longer the shot, the less you should open the clubface and the closer behind the ball the club should contact the sand. Therefore, set the clubface open a hair and focus on a spot about one inch behind the ball.

In the backswing, swing the club up to the three-quarter position, but avoid breaking your wrists too quickly. Delaying the wristcock cuts down the steepness of swing and height of the shot.

Rotating your right knee towards your left in the downswing will increase the pulling power of your hands, enabling you to drive the clubhead through the sand, with the force you need to send the ball flying lower and long enough.

Buried Ball Bail-Outs

The buried lie calls for a digging action, rather than a sliding action. Therefore, you must use a different club and an extra-steep technique, one that contrasts sharply with any other you'll use in the course of a round.

The pitching wedge features a narrow leading edge and is the perfect club for hitting either the long or short shot from a buried lie, because it enables you to knife the ball out of the sand.

To recover from this type of lie,

you must play the ball back and set up square, keeping your feet and body parallel to the target line. Also, hand action is now more critical than leg drive, so you can afford to dig your feet deeply into the sand.

Put more weight on your left foot to promote what should virtually be a straight up and down swinging action.

To get a clear picture of producing this action, incorporate the following image into your pre-swing visualisation process. Think of the action you use to splash a friend in the sea, this time when he is close to you. The base of your hand comes almost straight down and plunges into the water, so that the splash comes almost straight up into his face. You must use a similar technique to recover from a buried lie. The club swings almost straight up and down. The ball pops up.

Since the ball will come out "hotter", holding its line, you should set the clubface square to your target. Only open the blade when you have little green to work with, and need to swing with an out-to-in cutting across action.

Leaving your weight left, break your wrists immediately in the takeaway. Then swing the club straight back along the target line and up to the half-way point.

The key to the downswing is to

Two basic rules apply to sand play recovery: a level lie calls for a shallow cut of sand, while a buried ball, a deep cut.

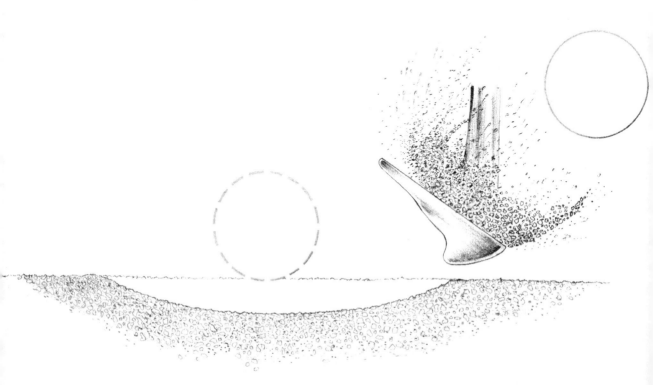

accelerate your hands, keeping them ahead of the clubhead, while your lower body makes a passive pass in the hitting area. So, don't be afraid to pull hard with your hands.

The club should contact the sand about a half-inch behind the ball if you have plenty of green to work with and about an inch behind if you don't.

WET SAND

If you are playing predominantly in Great Britain, you will face a lot of bunker shots from wet sand.

The wet texture can actually help the club slide through the sand. So, to compensate, move all your contact spots back a bit.

Of course, finding the spot that works for you takes some practice, largely due to everyone's tempo differing. So, don't be afraid to drop a few balls in the practice bunker, even if it's raining.

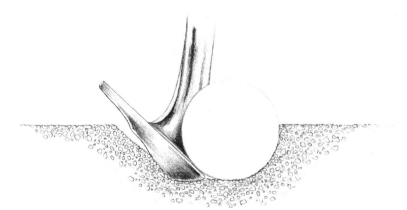

CHAPTER 12

PUTTING – LET YOUR ARMS AND SHOULDERS CONTROL THE STROKE

Perhaps, to you, putting looks simple; seemingly all a player makes is a wave of the putterblade on the way back and on the way through. As the ball rolls across the smooth, carpet-like surface, you probably wonder how it can possibly miss the cup.

Well, eventually, you won't wonder how the ball fails to fall into the hole. You'll see that putting *is* "another game". And that it is an art which you either do or do not have down to perfection from one stroke to the next.

Sometimes my putting stroke changes as quickly as a chameleon changes colour. Literally, one minute I've got the touch, the next minute I don't have a clue. Facing this reality, I'm left constantly searching for the answer. Nevertheless, I'm not alone.

Arnold Palmer says, "Putting looks easy, but isn't," and rummages daily through a garage littered with old putters, hoping one will come back to life.

Johnny Miller is now trying out an extra-long, 46-inch putter.

Isao Aoki adds tape to his putter one day, and removes it the next.

David Graham spends hours by the bending machine, adjusting the lie angle of his putter.

Denis Watson visits a sports psychologist. The list goes on.

When my ability to read the line is keen my confidence is in high gear and my stroke runs more or less on automatic. Stroking the ball in the hole is a snap. When I'm on form, I shoot at the flagsticks tucked in the tightest corners of the greens, knowing that if I miss my target and land in a trap or on the fringe, I can get up and down, thanks to a hot putter.

The other side of the coin: my game plan goes topsy-turvy when my stroke sours and I miss a knee-knocker early in the round, or watch a few balls peek in the hole and pop out, or take three putts. When things aren't going my way on the greens, I feel extra pressure to hit every approach shot close to the stick. And this monkey on my back causes me to think so much about technique that I steer the swing, instead of

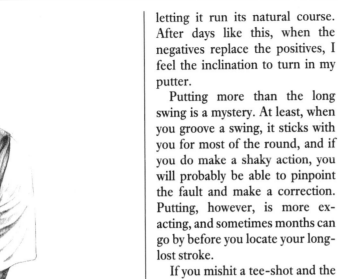

letting it run its natural course. After days like this, when the negatives replace the positives, I feel the inclination to turn in my putter.

Putting more than the long swing is a mystery. At least, when you groove a swing, it sticks with you for most of the round, and if you do make a shaky action, you will probably be able to pinpoint the fault and make a correction. Putting, however, is more exacting, and sometimes months can go by before you locate your long-lost stroke.

If you mishit a tee-shot and the ball lands in the rough, you can still hit your approach on the green. There are no second chances on the greens. I warn you: you will be aware of this fact every single time you step up to stroke a putt. The green will look like a snooker table's smooth green cloth. As you look at the hole, you will think there is only one truly acceptable result: to knock the ball in. This pressure is what causes you to miss. And when you fail to hole putt after putt, you become more nervous, and your stroke gets more and more tentative.

Virtually every Tour event I enter is won or lost on the greens. If I make birdie putts I have a good chance of winning, but if I three putt a few times, I expect to finish out of the big money. Following suit, your friendly matches will be decided on the smooth surfaces, too.

Putting nearly finished off Bernhard Langer, my German-born friend on Tour. He suffered from the "yips", a term golfers use to describe a jab-like stroke.

Langer changed to a heavier putter on the advice of Seve Ballesteros and decided to putt cross-handed, whenever the ball was inside 20 feet. Fortunately, the formula worked, but, mind you, the medicine didn't take effect overnight. Langer had to pay his dues, losing many tournaments while he was lifting himself out of the putting doldrums.

The style you use for putting doesn't matter all that much. Take Aoki, for example. He stoops over at address, plays the ball off the heel of the putter with the toe off the ground, and putts with an unconventional stabbing action. He does everything against the book, but is still one of the game's best putters. Bear in mind, he has putted this way all his life, has exceptional feel, and maybe even a pinch of God-given talent! I think if I "had" to putt like Aoki, I would probably have to consider looking into new career possibilities.

Hubert Green, the 1985 PGA champion, is another professional with an unusual style. He plays the ball off his right foot and grips the putter with a split-handed hold, yet his method works super. The number one reason why this is so: Green believes in his stroke. And a positive mental attitude is one of the keys to putting the ball into the hole.

Tom Watson, winner of five Open championships, was rated the world's top putter for a long time. Over the last few years, however, his putting game has lost some of its old fire. At first, he tried switching putters, but now he's back to an old model and trying to iron out faults in the stroke he still believes in.

As to my own prowess as a putter, switching from a wristy method to an arms and shoulders stroke has helped me in a big way. I found out the hard way that a wristy action needs to be perfectly timed in order to work, and when it breaks down, it is more difficult to repair than a pendulum stroke.

Only if I face a long putt, say 40 feet and upwards, will I incorporate a little wrist action into my stroke, to induce feel and to ensure I get the ball up to the hole. Otherwise, my method is wristless.

Aside from winning tournaments worldwide, on lightning-fast greens, standing second on the PGA Tour's 1988 putting statistics list, proved to me that my new putting stroke stands up to pressure better. I'm not saying that it will work every time. No stroke will. Studies by Dave Pelz, *Golf Magazine*'s technical consultant and former NASA scientist, show that if ten putts were rolled along the same line by a robot, they would not all drop, due to footprints, spike and ball marks.

It's facts like these that cause Gary Player to call putting "an inexact science".

Jack Nicklaus believes putting is "too important".

The immortal Ben Hogan still says: "There is no similarity between golf and putting – they are two different games – one played in the air, the other on the ground."

And old-timer Gene Sarazen, winner of all four Major championships, continues to cry out for a bigger cup.

Personally, I wish these facts about the robot weren't facts. In the meantime, I'll keep telling myself: "Sandy, the better your stroke, the better your chance of holing out."

My Stroke

I set up square, although if you see me open my stance slightly from time to time, don't be surprised, for as I've said, I'm always looking for "the" answer. I aim the putter-face at the hole, unless I'm allowing for borrow. (If that's the case, I set my body parallel to a point left or right of the hole and aim the face at that point.)

I hold the putter with a reverse overlap grip, resting my left forefinger across the first three fingers of my right hand, and put my left thumb straight down the centre of the shaft. Holding the putter in this fashion and weakening my left-hand grip takes my hands out of the stroke. My hands just hold on to the club – go along for the ride, so to speak.

I position the ball slightly right of my left heel, to allow the blade (which is naturally going to swing back a little on the inside) time to square itself up in the downswing, so, at impact, it is dead on line with the target.

I put 60 per cent of my weight on my left foot to encourage my body to stay steady and to accelerate the putterblade through the ball.

My most comfortable head position is one that allows me to look directly at the back of the ball with my left eye.

As to the position of my arms, I keep them close to my body, an adjustment that discourages any dramatic wavering of the putterblade on the back and through strokes.

One key I am a stickler for is the position of my left hand. Although I keep my hands "dead", or out of the stroke, I like to think that the back of my left hand is a secondary clubface. I know if I set up with the back of my left hand square to the target line, the blade is more likely to be perpendicular to the target line at impact.

In the backswing, I keep my head still, swing the putterblade low to the ground and keep my shoulders parallel to the target line.

In the through swing, I maintain the low blade position. To further encourage an accelerating action, I imagine that a coin is a few inches in front of the ball, and I try to brush it with the bottom of the putterblade.

Choosing a Putter

There are literally thousands of putters on the market. All these models fall into four basic types: centre shaft, mallet, blade, and off-set centre shaft. Each putter is either heavy or light, short or long, features a leather or rubber grip, a flat or upright lie.

I prefer a light-feeling, off-set centre shaft putter of standard length, featuring a leather grip and upright lie. But don't just copy me, for choosing a putter is very personal.

The flat putter usually suits the golfer who likes to keep his arms outstretched and his hands low.

Fuzzy Zoeller, the 1984 US Open champion, is an example of a player who prefers a flat putter, because he likes to give his arms more room to swing.

The upright putter best suits the tall golfer who stands close to the ball and prefers to set his hands high.

I like to stand up to the putt, therefore the upright lie is for me. However, Seve Ballesteros, who is also tall, likes to crouch over and prefers a "flattish" putter. So, you can see, these guidelines are not cast in bronze.

Choosing the right putter takes time and effort. The best approach is trial and error. Your

To groove a super-stroke: set up square to the target (1); Allow your arms and shoulders to swing the putterblade back low to the ground on an inside path (2); Keep your body relatively still as the blade returns to a square position (3); Then, allow the blade to swing through on the inside (4).

pro can point you in the right direction, but you are the only one who can determine which putter looks the best, feels the best and works the best.

Whichever putter you select – whether a brand-spanking-new model picked out of the pro-shop window, or an old beauty picked out of a barrel in your Aunt Ena's attic – make sure it gives you confidence and the feeling of balance throughout your stroke.

Another design feature that will help you limit your choice and allow you to putt better is the alignment marking. This line, dot, or arrow (not on all putters) helps you line up and, therefore, enables

you to hit putts that roll true to the line.

I think you can appreciate the facts: there are lots of variables to consider when choosing a putter. So, before you put your hard-earned pounds down on the pro's counter, wait until you stroke a few balls on the practice green and are happy with the results.

Draping your left forefinger over the first three fingers of your right hand and weakening your left-hand grip (so your thumb points straight down the shaft and the V points left of your chin) prevents you from making a "handsy" putting stroke.

FAST GREENS

Greens that are cut low, rolled, baked out by the sun, or hardened by the wind, can cause havoc to your putting touch, because the ball rolls quickly on such surfaces. You will probably find it easier to judge short downhill putts or to lag long putts close to the hole, if your putter is light.

I think a pendulum stroke will also help you putt consistently on fast greens. A stroke controlled by your arms and shoulders prevents you from snapping your wrists through impact and smacking the ball with your right hand, at the exact moment of impact. This fault causes you to run the ball several feet – or yards – by the hole.

On the other hand, some players I have spoken to believe the opposite is true. They claim that making a dead-handed stroke causes a player to lose his sense of touch on speedy greens. So, you see, there are few hard and fast rules.

Most players do agree that playing the ball close to the toe end of the putter and making a normal stroke, deadens the hit and prevents the golfer from stabbing putts on fast greens. When all is said and done, the best solution is for you to experiment on a slick surface, to see if this compensation is for you.

SLOW GREENS

I feel strongly that a heavy putter allows you to make a slower and smoother stroke on slow greens.

The tendency with a light putter on long or wet greens is to yank the blade back outside the target line, causing a "pull", or severely inside causing a "push".

To putt slow greens, try heeding the following tactics: 1. To set up for acceleration, put as much as 70 per cent of your weight on your left foot; 2. To help you hit the ball on the top half of the ball, for overspin, stand taller; 3. To help you control the movement of the putter, stand closer to the ball and, 4. Make a shorter backswing than normal and a longer follow-through to accelerate the putter through the ball and at the hole.

READING GREENS

For many years I determined which way the putt was going to break by only reading the slope from a position a few feet behind the ball. Recently, my reading ability has improved thanks to a four-point routine. Follow these steps and you will never be an "illiterate" putter.

1. Look at the way the green slopes as you approach the putting surface; 2. Walk around the side of the green to get a bird's-eye view from behind the cup, back to the ball; 3. Look at the putt from both side angles and, 4. Look at the putt from behind and try to mentally rehearse the ball rolling along a certain line into the cup.

If your playing partners are away, watch how their putts roll and, more importantly, how hard a stroke they put on the ball. Now, you are ready to hole out.

PUTTING IN WIND

A strong headwind can disturb your stroke and do tricks with a ball putted slowly across a smooth surface. So take precautions:

● Widen your stance for better balance.

● Bend more from the knees for better leverage.

● Choke down on the grip for easier control of the putterblade.

● Make a shorter, but firmer stroke.

PART 5

SHOTMAKING

CHAPTER 13

AROUND, OVER AND UNDER TROUBLE – LET YOUR IMAGINATION RUN WILD

Every golfer's dream is to play one perfect round. Ironically, neither the swing nor the game was designed for total perfection or predictability. I thank the golfing gods for sticking to such a masterful plan; if I knew I was going to hit a cracker every time I stood up to the ball, and that every bounce was going to go in my favour, I wouldn't play golf. The game would bore me to tears.

You'll want the game to challenge you, too; recovering from a bad shot or bad break is part of golf's intrigue.

The single-figure player knows this. Able to hit a draw or fade, he can shorten dogleg holes by working the ball around the corner. Able to send the ball flying high or low, he can hit greens from troublespots.

I'm confident that you can develop these same shotmaking skills, providing you learn the causes and effects of a particular setup and swing. The real secret, however, is to let your imagination run wild. Visualise the shot curv-ing, shooting over or under trees, and you will turn fantasy into reality. The thrill of seeing your shot happen is your reward for practice, patience, perseverance and preswing planning.

During my junior days, I was on the practice tee at Hawkstone Park, trying to hit a draw, using a method that is commonly advo-cated: strong grip, closed stance, flat swing, and quick release of the hands through impact.

My father, who as it turned out was watching me, could see that I wasn't having much success. He came running out of the house, grabbed the club out of my hand and said, sternly, "Sandy, that's not the way to hit a draw, that is the way to hit a duck hook!"

I'm thankful that he stayed on the tee for a couple of hours, showing me the fundamentals for working the ball.

Even my father concedes, however, that tuning in on the proper technique is not enough to manoeuvre the ball. The more you play golf, the more automatic be-comes the setup and swing. This sounds like sweet news, but it isn't. When human beings hear the word automatic, they usually become lax. I'm no exception. So, to prevent myself from falling asleep at the wheel, so to speak, I have to play mental movies of the shot I want to play. Incorporating a positive picture into my address rehearsal is especially important if I want to make the ball dance in the air. I picture some crazy im-ages, but they work. They will help you, too, so try not to fear them. Let your mind wander, your im-agination run wild.

I'd like to think that everyone's images are unique, so you won't necessarily value from copying mine. But there is no harm in trying. Aside from that, by know-ing what my favourite mental movies are, you will be more com-fortable with your own, and be more apt to think up several that will enable you to hit a draw, fade, high or low shot.

Hitting a Draw

MY MENTAL MOVIE: I picture a racing cyclist pedalling around the right hand bank of an oval track, in a counterclockwise direction. Thus, the right-to-left shape of a draw.

Your Technique

In all probability, your natural shot will be a fade. Nevertheless, the quicker you learn how to draw the ball, the quicker you will shave strokes off your score.

To reiterate, the draw will come in handy when playing a tee-shot on a hole that doglegs left. But there are more advantages. Perfecting this shot will also enable you to pick up extra yards when playing into a strong wind. And if you possess the talent to hit the draw, you will be able to curl the ball around trouble.

To make the ball curve left, rather subtly, align your feet and shoulders to the right of your target, or parallel to the line you want the ball to start its flight pattern on.

Set the clubface closed, aiming it where you want the ball to finish. The more draw flight you want to impart on the ball, the more you close the face and the farther right you align your body.

Swinging the club along the path set up by your shoulders enables the ball to start its flight to the right, while the closed clubface imparts spin on the ball, drawing it back to the target.

Caution: The closed clubface causes the ball to run farther with overspin, once it touches down. Compensate for this result by taking one "less" club.

Hitting a Fade

MY MENTAL MOVIE: I picture a train moving along a set of tracks that curve "quietly" around a bend, from left to right. This image matches the subtle left-to-right ball flight I want to impart on the ball.

Your Technique

The simplest way to fade the ball is to point your shoulders and feet left of your ultimate target, open the clubface and swing normally. The bigger the fade you want to hit, the farther left you align your body and the more you open the clubface. Yes, it's that simple. Yes, the technique is virtually opposite to the one you use to hit a draw.

You'll find that hitting a fade with one of the longer clubs in your bag is easier than playing a fade with a short iron, simply because the long clubs feature straighter faces with less loft. Therefore, they work across the ball and not underneath it. The result: more sidespin.

To prevent hitting a shot farther into trouble on the right with a long club, you will need to compensate by aiming more drastically to the left than you would if you had a short club in your hand.

Caution: The cutting swing you make will add loft to the club and chop off some distance. This will show up more in the medium and short irons. Allow for this by taking one "more" club.

Hitting a High Shot

MY MENTAL MOVIE: I picture a firework rocket flying up into a night sky, over the trees and descending slowly, as a parachutist falls. This positive image boosts my confidence, helping me hit the high shot.

Your Technique

No matter how fine a player you become, you're bound to knock a ball off line and have to carry tall trees. Have no fear, achieving extra height with any club is easy.

Simply, play the ball forward in your stance, with your hands slightly behind, to increase the effective loft of the clubface, which should be open slightly. Then, just swing back normally.

In the downswing, keep most of your weight back, on your right foot, and your head behind the ball, to help you make contact on the upswing.

Hitting a Low Shot

MY MENTAL MOVIE: I picture a sharpshooter, lying down behind my ball, firing a low rifle shot. This image matches the low-ball flight I want to accomplish.

Your Technique

Knowing how to execute a low-flying shot is a big advantage, especially if overhanging branches obstruct your line to the green.

The high handicap golfer is under the false impression that this shot requires a forceful action. In trying to keep the ball down, he uses too much upper body in the downswing. The steep angle of descent causes the ball to rise, rather than fly low. And because he tends to "come over the top" with his upper body, the ball usually flies left of the target, to boot.

Don't you make those same mistakes. Position the ball back in your stance, so your hands are ahead, and put a touch more weight on your left foot.

Keeping your weight left and lower body relatively still, make a wider extension in the takeaway, then swing the club up no higher than the three-quarter position.

Activate your knees a little to start the downswing, and let your hands lead the clubhead into the back of the ball.

CHAPTER 14

WIND – DON'T EVER FIGHT THE BREEZES

Breezy days are as common a condition on inland courses as blustery days on a seaside links.

On links courses, the inward and outward holes usually run in opposite directions. If you're lucky, you'll play both sides with the wind at your back, due to a sudden change in direction. However, if the golfing gods are in a morose mood, you might find yourself battling a stiff breeze on both the front nine and homeward half. So, be prepared to battle the wind if you visit Scotland, England or Ireland for a golf vacation.

Practising and playing so often in everchanging conditions, I consider my ability to beat the wind to be my greatest golfing asset. This skill has already allowed me to chalk up victories all over the world, including of course the 1985 British Open Championship. And, since the "Open" is always contested over a seaside links, let me say out of pride that I reckon my chances of picking up this premier title again are pretty good indeed.

The real knack of knocking the ball down under the wind, controlling its flight when playing down-wind or in a crosswind, took me years to learn, but you can do more than get by on a windy course, anywhere in the world, if you groove the basic swing techniques that I'm about to spell out. After that, becoming an expert is all about building confidence by playing wind shots over and over again.

When the Wind is Against You

Watching golfers trying to belt the ball into the wind and nearly falling over in the process, is a familiar sight at any course, on any Saturday or Sunday morning.

Surprisingly, the headwind is the simplest condition to conquer, yet the typical weekend golfer struggles because he swings the club speedily and on too steep a plane. The combination of a quick pick-up backswing and a sharp descending blow imparted on the ball causes a high shot, just what the doctor *didn't* order.

Playing the ball too far back in the stance, anywhere beyond the midway point, is what makes the swing arc too narrow. So, play the ball a few inches to the right of your left heel.

The key to hitting shots that pierce the wind is "penetration" – putting the clubface squarely on the ball, then driving the clubhead low to the ground in the follow-through. This motion enables you to sweep the longer clubs, and to take "bacon strip" (not "pork chop") divots with the short and medium irons.

Swing simplicity is the key to achieving penetration. You don't want to overdo body movement by swaying off the ball and you don't want to swing fast. To achieve a penetrating blow, all you have to do on the way back is move the club away slowly with a longer one-piece extension (the key to achieving a wide arc), and make a strong shoulder turn, as you swing up to the three-quarter position. All you have to do on the way down is maintain a deep knee flex (an aid to balance and leverage) and allow your hands to lead the clubhead into, and through, the ball.

The secret of hitting piercing short- and medium-iron shots into a strong wind is to exaggerate the actions of swinging the club back and through, along the target line.

Visualising taking a "bacon strip" divot (not a "pork chop" divot) will encourage the proper technique.

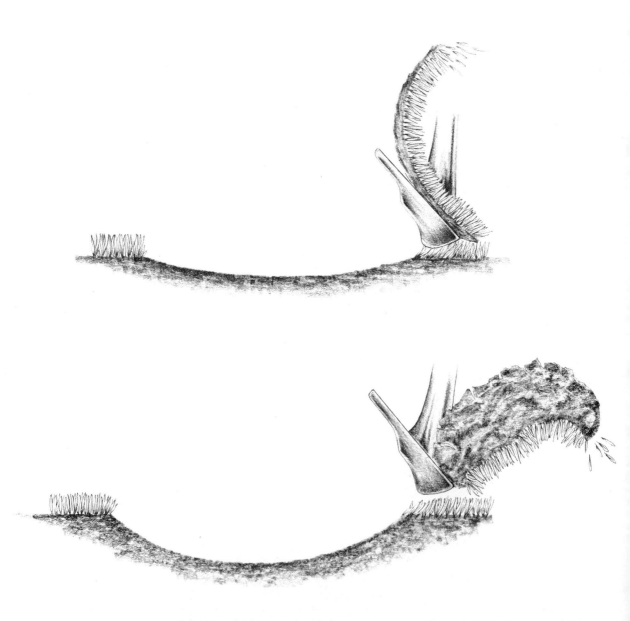

HIGH TEE

If your drives fly on a high trajectory into the wind, tee the ball a bit higher. Yes, that's right. The elevated tee promotes the flattish swing you need to zoom the ball down the fairway, regardless of the windy wall in front of you.

Teeing up so the ball is below the top of the clubface, or even level with it, promotes a steep swing – an action that causes the ball to "balloon" in the air. So, tee up so that half of the ball is "above" the top of the clubface.

ADVANCED TIP FOR CHEATING THE WIND

No doubt, you've heard the expression, "There's more than one way to skin a cat". Well, you can apply this same philosophy to golf.

Let me share a secret with you single-figure players who have the sweeping action down to a science, but still feel scared swinging a driver on a narrow par-four, when a strong headwind prevails.

Don't panic: you can hit a ball on a string and pick up 20 more yards by playing a one-iron, providing you purposely play a "flier". Here's how:

1. Instead of putting the ball on a peg, build your own tee by digging the heel of your shoe into the ground, as a rugby player does when preparing to kick a goal.

2. Then set the ball on the little home-made mound you've constructed, so a few blades of grass lie between the ball and the clubface. (The grass serves as the catalyst in producing the flier), and

3. Now, just swing normally and watch the ball shoot off the clubface and "cheat" the wind.

ENOUGH CLUB

Picking the proper club can be baffling when hitting iron shots into the wind, so here's a quick tip that should help you make the right choice and get the ball up to the hole.

For every 10 m.p.h. of wind, take one more club. Let's say you face a 130-yard shot in a 30 m.p.h. headwind. If you normally hit a seven iron, play a four. All you have to do now is make a compact swing and chase the ball with the clubface through impact.

When the Wind is With You

Playing down-wind is a confidence booster. This condition generally makes life easier, but it has its tricky aspects. First, let's look at the easy side of hitting shots when the wind is at your back.

If you're looking to achieve added length from the tee or the fairway, by letting the ball "ride" the wind, all you have to do is: 1. Play the ball forward in your stance, directly opposite your left heel, or even a hair in front of this spot; 2. Put 60 per cent of your weight on your right foot; 3. Make a looser and more upright back-swing and, 4. Coming down, keep your head behind the ball to help you make clubface-to-ball contact on the upswing.

The tricky part of playing shots down-wind is thinking strategically. Sometimes, the average weekend golfer smashes a driver off the tee, or plays a lay-up second shot with an iron, to a par five, without concentrating on the hazards up ahead.

With a strong wind at your back, you can hit into hazards you never reached before. Nevertheless, if you take precautions during your preswing routine, you can make out like a bandit.

Throwing up a few blades of grass and watching how the wind blows them, looking at the leaves moving, or at the flag blowing, if you can see it, will give you some indication of the wind's strength. If you think there is any chance that you can reach trouble off the tee, leave the driver in your bag and reach for a fairway wood. When hitting a lay-up shot with an iron, play one less club for every 10 m.p.h. of following wind.

THE "KNOCKDOWN" SHOT

Occasionally, you'll face a short-iron shot into a green featuring no trouble in front, with a strong wind at your back. Because it's difficult to stop the ball on the green in these conditions, I suggest you play a "knockdown" – a shot that flies under the wind, lands short of the green and rolls up to the hole.

To hit this shot: 1. Play the ball in the middle of your stance; 2. Put a touch more weight on your left foot; 3. Choke down on the club for control; 4. Extend the club in the take-away; 5. Maintain a shallow plane and swing up to the half-way point, and 6. Consciously lead the clubhead with your hands through impact.

One footnote: Club selection will vary because swing tempo differs from player to player. Your playing partner may hit a knockdown seven-iron shot from 150 yards, while you may need to play a five from the same distance in order to reach the green. Because I can't help you here, you will have to experiment.

Crosswinds

Crosswinds used to give me the most problems because I had a habit of trying to get "cute". I would hook the ball into a left-to-right wind, or fade the ball in the opposite condition. Unfortunately, lots of times the wall of wind didn't hold my ball up, and my shot finished through the green. So, I gave up fighting the wind and adopted a more sensible approach: letting the wind blow the ball back to my target. And, if you want to save yourself shots and frustration, you should follow suit.

Once you determine the wind's direction and strength, your strategy is all about aiming. If the wind is blowing from left to right, set your body and the clubface square to the point you think the ball must start out on, then hit to that target, and let the wind blow the ball back to the flag. When the crosswind blows in the opposite direction, use the same strategy.

Only if you find yourself hitting through the "starter" target and into trouble left or right should you change your clubface position. In a left-to-right wind, open the face slightly to help the ball float back to the target. In the opposite wind, close the face a hair. Otherwise, don't play games. Gimmicks never work on the golf course.

PART 6

DEVILISH LIES

CHAPTER 15

ON HILLS – SWING WITH THE SLOPE, NOT AGAINST IT

It's inevitable that you will face severe uphill, downhill, and sidehill lies on the links courses of Great Britain and Ireland. Such lies are not as common on most American courses, but you'll run into these "beauties" somewhere, sometime, so be prepared. Look at these shots as challenges. After all, awkward lies have been part of the game's history, ever since the first shots were hit off the undulating fairways of St Andrews.

The high handicap player panics when facing such on-course predicaments, simply because he knows he is unprepared. He doesn't bother to learn and practise the proper techniques involved, because he figures he'll only run into a truly tricky lie once during a round. And if the golfing gods are on his side, maybe he will be lucky enough to play all eighteen holes without having to hit one shot off a hilly lie. What's more, in the past, he's probably been able to recover thirty per cent of the time, by virtue of fate, improvisa-

tion or, to his credit, by using common sense. Consequently, he's willing to take his chances.

By adopting this attitude, he's treating golf as he would a lottery. If the shot comes off, jolly good, if not, that's okay, too. I have nothing against a golfer who plays with this outlook, providing he doesn't cry in his beer at the 19th, blaming a hilly lie for a high score on a hole.

Those who do complain fail to accept the facts: the only way to recover consistently well from hilly lies is to learn the various methods, and to practise them over and over.

I acknowledge those who argue that it's difficult to practise hilly lies. Yes, often one's local courses are flat. And if a course does feature rolling fairways, it is usually too crowded for members to hit shots off hilly spots, or the club forbids such on-course practising. All the same, I am still a strong supporter of that well-known cliché, "Where there's a will, there's a way."

Booking a lesson with your local

pro, going to a tournament and watching pros hit shots off slopes, or viewing their techniques on television, are all excellent alternatives to sitting on one's bum.

The fact that you are reading *Learning Golf: The Lyle Way* shows you are really making an effort to learn the game – the right way. And I am sure it will pay off.

In the instruction that follows, I address the problem of not being able to practise hilly lies by giving you ways to simulate uphill and downhill slopes. Along with these tips, I'll teach you how to recover from sidehill lies and include more than one method.

Uphill Lie

The common error that the average golfer makes when playing a shot off an uphill lie is to leave his weight on his right foot in the downswing. The reason: a faulty setup. Consequently, he loses his balance, sways off the ball in the backswing, and unable to swing the club down smoothly with his

arms, he makes a desperate flick at the ball with his hands, hitting a pull.

Setting up with the ball just about midway in your stance, and aiming your body to the right (more when the slope's severe), will help solve the problem of hitting the ball left of the target. The number one key, however, for playing shots off this type of lie is to tilt your body to your right, at address, so that it is at right angles to the slope. By setting up in this fashion, in effect, you give yourself a flat lie.

Flexing your left knee drastically, and bracing your right leg, are important features of the setup, too, for they serve as aids to balance, and build a firm foundation.

Naturally, from this setup position, leg and hip action will be restricted, but that's a plus, because you will need to swing the club, essentially, with your arms.

If you settle into a severe slope correctly, and make allowances for the pull, by aiming right, and for a high flight by taking one more club, you will automatically swing the club low going back, up the slope coming through, and come out of this troublespot "smelling like a rose".

Simulating the Uphill Slope

To develop an awareness of the desired ascending angle of the swing, place a range ball bucket or a wooden crate under your left foot.

Practising wood and iron shots from this awkward position will give you a feel for the correct swinging action. In no time, you'll build confidence and be able to conquer the course, even if every other shot is off an uphill lie.

Downhill Lie

Again, the solution to the problem of playing this shot is to tilt yourself perpendicular to the slope.

There are numerous ways to hit the ball off this type of lie, but through trial-and-error, I think I have discovered the simplest, and most foolproof method. In a nutshell, here it is:

With the ball played back, stand open, and set the clubface open a hair to offset the tendency to hit a pull.

Allowing your wrists to be lively, swing the club back on an upright plane, with your hands and arms.

Swing the club down with the slope and stay with the shot, by maintaining your knee flex and "chasing" the ball with the clubhead, through impact.
NOTE: If you prefer to keep the clubface square at address, play one less club, as the ball back position causes your hands to be ahead of the ball, and the clubface to be delofted.

Simulating the Downhill Slope

To familiarise yourself with downhill lies, place an object under your right foot, and hit several balls with several clubs. Start by using a short bucket, then put a higher object under your foot to increase the severity of the slope and the steepness of the swing.

Sidehill Lie: Ball Above Feet

Off this kind of lie, the tendency is for the ball to move from right to left. So take precautions straight away: aim the clubface and your body to the right of target.

Choke down on the club for control, and set your weight more towards your toes to help you retain balance.

The lie itself will make you swing flatter, but it will not hurt to paint a picture in your mind of a sweeping action in the hitting area.

The entire swing should be governed by your hands and arms, so keep your left foot firmly planted and the rest of your body pretty still throughout the action. NOTE: There's another way to play this shot: set up square to your target with the clubface open a hair, and make a normal swing.

If you like the sound of this method, take one more club than normal because the ball will not come out as "hot".

Sidehill Lie: Ball Below Feet

It's easy to stand up on this shot, a split second before impact, and to top the ball as a result. Therefore, you must protect against this fault at address by bending more at the knees.

The ball will tend to fade off this lie, so allow for this flight by aiming your body and the clubface to the left of target.

Standing closer to the ball, which should be positioned in the middle of your stance, will put you in a "control" position, and promote a more upright swing plane.

To preserve your balance, set your weight on your heels, and make a shorter more compact backswing.

In the downswing, transfer your weight back to your left foot, try to retain your exaggerated knee flex, and keep your head still, as you pull the club into the back of the ball.

NOTE: Alternate method: set your body parallel to the target line, but close the clubface, more or less, depending on the severity of the slope. If it is really falling away from you, close it more.

Then, make a short, but fluid swing.

CHAPTER 16

IN ROUGH – BRAINS ARE BETTER THAN BRAWN

Naturally, since I'm a rather big bloke, golf enthusiasts, such as yourself, probably think that sheer power is what allows me to sail the ball out of the "thick stuff" bordering the fairways. The truth is, I rarely muscle the ball.

Only if I'm in a "do or die" situation against a match play opponent, and the ball is sitting down deeply in the grass, a long way from the green, will I put my swing into high gear, and give it one. In most instances, I depend more on brains than brawn: choosing the correct club for the job, sticking to a simple technique, and knowing when to play a percentage shot up the fairway, in a position for a pitch and putt, is the essence of my recovery power.

Having frequently been paired with high handicap players in pro-am tournaments, I've had the opportunity to watch them at work in the rough. Sadly, no matter how poor the lie, they adhere to one basic philosophy: Go for broke.

I appreciate that most of these players are out for a day's enjoy-ment, so I don't come down hard on them during play. But after finishing nine holes, or the round, I will try to give them some guidance, based on my own experiences – if they ask for it. I figure, if they truly want to improve, they will do that. And most of the time, I'm right. When I ask, "Would you dream of fishing for marlin with a bamboo pole, or shooting a wild elephant with a pellet pistol?" and they answer with a point-blank, "No", they realise what I'm getting at. I am trying to tell them in a nice way that a long iron is the wrong equipment to use when trying to extract a golf ball out of rough. Some of them know this, but depend on "hope" to shoot a decent score. Unfortunately, these golfers will never learn. They want to make magic, without studying the tricks of the trade.

Others are simply inexperienced, as I once was, and are willing to listen and learn. Obviously, your reading Learning Golf: The Lyle Way shows you are anxious to pick up some pointers. So, let's get on with today's lesson.

If lifting the ball out of thick rough and advancing it up the fairway is your objective, and you're too close to the green to hit a wood, hitting a punch with a short-medium iron is the "call". To play it, simply position the ball back in your stance, close the clubface a hair to allow for the thick grass twisting the blade open, and swing on a more vertical plane to hit with a sharp descending blow.

This steep swing is the one I use most from rough, but my technique will vary from situation to situation, as should yours. To prove my point, let's say you face a short-iron approach into a green, and there is grass between the ball and the clubface. Confronting this lie, you must first defend against the ball "flying" as much as 20 yards more than normal and landing with overspin. How? By using a special technique, and taking one more club.

To accomplish height and biting action from a "flier" lie: 1. Move the ball forward in an open stance; 2. Open the clubface

slightly and; 3. Swing the club on the normal inside-square-inside path, but incorporate lively wrist action into your technique, so your hands work the clubface under the ball.

Facing a longer shot to the green, and getting the ball to sit down quietly, can also be accomplished without muscling the ball. The deeper the ball sits in the rough, the less effective long irons become, because the grass grabs hold of the thin clubhead and twists the face open or closed. A lofted wood will slide through the grass without slowing down or twisting off line. And if you play a soft fade, the ball will sit down softly on the putting surface.

To hit this particular shot from rough, start off by playing the ball back a couple of inches in an open stance, to programme steepness into your technique, and stand a touch taller than normal to encourage your arms to control the swinging action.

Set the blade open a hair, to programme left-to-right flight into the shot, and grip more firmly to retain this clubface position at impact.

Now, just swing back on a steep angle and pull the club down into the back of the ball with your hands.

You can see that playing shots from rough requires versatility. This is why it is critical to learn various techniques. Ignore this advice and you will be a robotistic one-swing golfer and suffer when the ball scoots into the heavy grass.

Practising long and short shots from the worst lies imaginable is the best form of training. Quite frankly, this is the only way you can become a "smooth" player from rough, capable of surprising an opponent with your ability to recover. However, to give you a start in building a full repertoire of shots, I'll review several course situations and give you some quick tips that vary slightly from those I've already covered.

LIE: Ball buried in grassy uphill slope, 20–30 feet from the flagstick.

TECHNIQUE: With the ball positioned opposite your left heel, set your feet, hips and shoulders parallel to the target line.

The uphill lie will probably prevent you from planting your left foot firmly, so lean into the slope. Grip down on the shaft for control and close the clubface slightly to compensate for the blade opening when it contacts the grass.

Keeping your wrists firm and weight left, swing the club back in one piece to knee height.

Now, pull the clubface down with both hands, blasting the ball from the grass. The ball will pop out, land softly, and roll slowly towards the hole.

LIE: Ball down in rough, 30 yards from a pin cut close behind the edge of a bunker.

TECHNIQUE: Don't get cute; your priority is to carry the bunker and to land the ball somewhere on the green.

With the ball positioned forward in your stance, align your body left of the target and open the clubface of a sand wedge to programme loft into the shot.

Keeping your left arm stiffer than normal and allowing your right wrist to cock immediately in the takeaway, swing the club back to the half-way position.

Pull the club down with both hands, and driving your right shoulder under your chin, allow the clubhead to contact the grass about an inch behind the ball. Exaggerate the follow-through to help propel the ball upward.

LIE: Ball in heather, 150 yards from the green.

TECHNIQUE: Unless you catch a lucky lie that allows you to "go after" the ball, refrain from becoming overly aggressive in heather. If you try to pulverise the ball, it will take more than a Herculean effort to prevent the clubhead from turning the second it contacts the tangly rough.

So when facing a "hairy" in the heather, you should usually play the ball back safely to the fairway with a pitching wedge. This club is not as lofted as the sand iron but, featuring a sharper leading edge and less bounce, it is ideal for the job.

With the ball back, stand open and put as much as 70 per cent of your weight on your left foot.

With the blade set open, hover the club above the heather, because the slightest touch will cause the ball to move out of position in this springy texture.

Gripping tightly, swing the club almost straight up, and down again, controlling the action with your hands and arms. Through impact, keep your hands ahead of the clubhead, otherwise you will run the risk of shutting the blade. And you will be playing another shot from heather.

LIE: Ball in semi-rough, 130 yards from the green. Overhanging limbs block your line.

TECHNIQUE: Only if the match is on the line, and you have to get the ball on the green, should you try this shot. Otherwise, play out safely to the fairway.

First, visualise the shot. Don't swing until you have seen the ball fly under the branches, land, and run on to the putting surface.

With the ball played in the middle of your stance, distribute your weight equally between the ball and heel of each foot. Set your hands ahead of the ball and hood the face of a four iron to ensure a low trajectory and plenty of roll.

Keeping your lower body almost perfectly still, and wrist action minimal, swing your hands back to chest height, moving the club inside the target line.

Now, swing the club down and drive the clubhead low to the ground through impact.

CHAPTER 17

IN SAND – DON'T LET THE LIE SCARE YOU INTO SUBMISSION

Regardless of all the hundreds of competitive rounds I have under my belt, I still run into lies that shake me up – in the sand, usually.

There are days when I stand in a bunker, shaking my head. Sizing up the lie, I turn to my regular Tour caddie Dave Musgrove, saying: "Blimey, I don't think I know how to hit this shot."

"Thanks, Sandy," I can hear you say. "You're teaching me how to play golf, and you don't even know how to hit every shot in the bag."

Now, wait just a minute. This is a fact, I don't know how to play "all" the shots. But, in all fairness, who does? No golfer alive can predict how awkward a lie he will face on a particular day. And, occasionally, the ball nestles itself in a position that I never dreamed was possible.

What I do when facing such a puzzling lie is the same thing you should do: regroup by taking a couple of deep breaths, analyse the situation carefully, and muster up a shot based on intuition and imagination.

Often, from such predicaments, simply putting the ball on the green requires a minor miracle. So, be honest about what type of sand shot you think you are capable of hitting.

No matter how many rounds you play and how imaginative your practice is, inevitably you will run into strange lies in the sand. Nevertheless, practising peculiar bunker shots is pretty good preventive medicine, for it lessens the odds of facing a "doozie".

This is why American pros are capable of pulling off what looks to be the "impossible". I'll let you in on a secret: there's no magic involved, and rarely are their backs really up against the wall.

During practice, U.S. Tour players put themselves in predicaments. In the bunker, they play shots off severe downhill slopes, out of buried lies – you name it. Hence, they are ready as they can be for surprises out on the course.

As Lee Trevino says, "There's no use wasting your time practising shots that you can hit with your eyes closed, you have to practise and teach yourself to hit shots you can't hit with your eyes open."

This advice has helped me prepare for the unpredictable. Granted, this kind of practice is pretty sophisticated and, perhaps, geared more to the single-figure golfer who has grooved the basic bunker play techniques, and has more time to work on fancier shots. Still and all, spending even fifteen minutes each weekend hitting shots from "cute" lies in the sand can only make you a more complete golfer.

Three lies that will give you the heebie-jeebies, unless you practise recovering from them, are: 1. Ball sitting on a downhill slope, in a bunker, 2. Ball buried in a bunker wall and, 3. Ball in a relatively high-lipped fairway bunker.

Without pretending to be able to predict your future, I know you will eventually run into these lies, maybe even on your first trip around the course. Don't panic. Here are some tips that might help you turn fright into fruition.

Ball Sitting on a Downhill Slope

Playing this type of bunker shot requires a slightly different action from when the ball is sitting on a similar slope in the fairway. On the "short grass", you are worried most about contacting the ball cleanly, and less concerned about finesse. This is not the case in the sand, where you have several considerations: 1. The distance to the flag; 2. The tilt of the green; 3. The texture of the sand; 4. Where to land the ball on the putting surface; 5. The speed of swing; 6. The length of your backswing and, 7. The length of your follow-through.

When playing a downhill sand shot to a pin close to the edge of the trap, with the green sloping towards the hole, your first order of business is to conjure up some confidence. Visualise the club-head cutting the sand, the ball carrying the lip, landing on the edge of the green, and rolling towards the hole. Also, you want to discourage a long follow-through, so imagine a solid-steel wall, a couple of feet in front of the ball. If the club hits the wall, you will hurt your hands.

Once you trigger the preswing routine by seeing the shot, wiggle your feet into the sand. Then, playing the ball in the middle of your stance, instead of back, as you would if the ball were on a downhill slope in the fairway, set your body slightly open to the target. And be sure to bend your knees, considerably.

Playing the ball too far back and standing too open will only cause you to contact the sand too quickly in the downswing. And that spells trouble with a capital T.

Failing to increase your knee flex will prompt you to stand up in the hitting area. The result: a "skull".

Holding the club with a "weak" grip will encourage a vertical backswing plane, while setting the clubface open will allow you to take a thinner slice of sand.

Choking down on the handle and swinging back to the half-way position will promote control.

Coming down, you must not get overaggressive by getting over-anxious with the hands. Keeping your knees super-flexed, maintaining a slow tempo, swinging the club into the sand about an inch behind the ball and stunting the follow-through action, are keys you must work on.

I have to emphasise the importance of maintaining knee flex in the hitting area. If the knees are allowed to rotate too actively, the upper body reacts in the same way. The right forearm turns over, so does the hand, so does the club-face. Do this, and you'll send the ball "screaming" across the green. Once again, knees flexed, forearms parallel at impact.

If the texture of the sand is a trifle more firm, hit farther behind the ball with a pitching wedge (open blade) and dig the ball out.

Ball Buried in Bunker Wall

When the ball is buried just below

the front lip of a bunker, you have to face one fact: nine out of ten times you are not going to hit the ball stiff to the hole, especially if the flag is a long way away. Sure, this is strong medicine to swallow, but failing to come to terms with this fact, and getting greedy in the process, will cause you to grind your teeth with anger, for, no doubt, you will leave the ball in the sand.

Everything is relative. You have heard this phrase before, I'm sure, but let me tell you how it applies to this situation. Results take on a new perspective. Hitting a "great" recovery shot now means putting the ball anywhere on the green. Hitting an "extra, extra-spectacular" recovery shot means putting the ball next to the stick. If you are tempted to go for the spectacular, remind yourself that if you leave the ball in the bunker, it's "curtains". Think strategically: if you land the ball anywhere on the green, you still have a chance to make a putt.

To recover from this lie, you have to:

1 Play the ball back in a square-to-slightly-open stance. Yes, here you want the ball back, because you *want* to catch the ball early in the downswing and dig deeper into the sand. This is the only way to lift the ball from this lie.

2 Bury both feet into the sand, straighten your right leg, so much so that it feels like an iron post, and put more weight on your right foot. Burying your feet promotes an arm swing. Bracing your right leg discourages any faulty swaying action of the body. Putting pressure on your right foot encourages you to contact the ball early in the downswing.

3 Lay the blade back, so it faces skyward. This will give you enough loft to carry the bunker wall.

4 Allowing your wrist action to be lively, swing the club straight back along the target line and up to the half-way position, coiling your upper body. Yes, you're right, I told you to avoid a big coiling action when playing bunker shots. However, this is no ordinary shot. Here, you need power to extract the ball. And turning the upper body is how you generate that power.

5 Keeping your head steady, pull the club down as hard as you damn well can, driving the blade deeply into the sand, hitting a spot close behind the ball. To help you stay behind the ball during the downswing, use the following mental image that I picked up, years ago, from former Open champion, Henry Cotton: try to peek under the ball as you swing the blade down, into the sand.

Ball Sitting in a Fairway Bunker (the "Augusta" Shot)

If there's one swing thought to key on when playing a full shot from a fairway bunker, it's to hit the ball before the sand. This is opposite to the normal strategy in sand, but, remember, you want to advance the ball up the fairway or on to a green that sits usually 150 yards away.

Before you step into the sand, determine which is the least lofted club that will get you over the lip. Then take one more club, for the shot I'm teaching you imparts fading action on the ball, so it rises quickly, flies higher, and doesn't go as far.

Playing the ball back in your stance, closer to your right foot, will enable you to contact the ball before the swing levels out and the clubface squares up. You want the clubface to be slightly open at impact to help you lift the ball.

Taking an open stance and putting more weight on your left foot will encourage you to make a steep three-quarter backswing, while planting your feet into the sand prevents any slipping and sliding.

Since your leg action will be restricted due to your feet being buried, your upper body is bound to get ahead of your lower body in the downswing. "But won't I tend to swing across the ball?" you probably are asking yourself. Yes, you will. But this is what you want to do, in order to achieve higher flight and bite.

How do you start down, where does the power come from? You start down by lowering the knees and putting pressure on the balls of your feet. This leverage action will enable you to generate power by increasing the speed of your arm swing. Keep your hands ahead of the clubhead in the hitting area and your head behind the ball until after the hit, and the only question you'll have to ask is: "How close is it?"

PART 7

ON THE LINKS

CHAPTER 18

THE LIE OF THE LAND – LOCAL KNOWLEDGE AND LEARNING TO SCORE GO HAND IN HAND

At least half the fun of playing golf is beating the course, even if it's just on one hole. Before you can appreciate exactly what I mean by this, you must learn the characteristics of a typical layout, whether a course is a modern-day man-made design, or essentially the work of Mother Nature, as is the famed St Andrews links in Scotland. Once you do, you'll know what you're up against.

Your typical course comprises 18 holes, and each one of these is either a par three, four or five. Par varies according to yardage and is the score a scratch player is expected to shoot on a hole.

MEN'S PAR	
Par 3:	250 yards and under
Par 4:	251–475 yards
Par 5:	476 yards and over

WOMEN'S PAR	
Par 3:	200 yards and under
Par 4:	201–400 yards
Par 5:	401 yards and over

Most courses on my side of the Atlantic average 6,500 yards in total length, and are par 69 or 70. Not surprisingly, American layouts are longer; many stretch out to 7,000-plus yards and play to a par of 72.

As you will discover, the shorter course is not always the easiest to score on. How difficult a layout is depends on the number and severity of a myriad of hazards. Bunkers, water, tall trees, treacherous rough, heather, and high winds (that can turn the shortest and tamest course into a terrifying animal) will all put your shotmaking skills to a test.

The philosophy of scoring is straightforward: if you plan your strategy carefully and avoid the trouble that lurks, you can shoot a score of par or better. If not, you will score a bogey or worse.

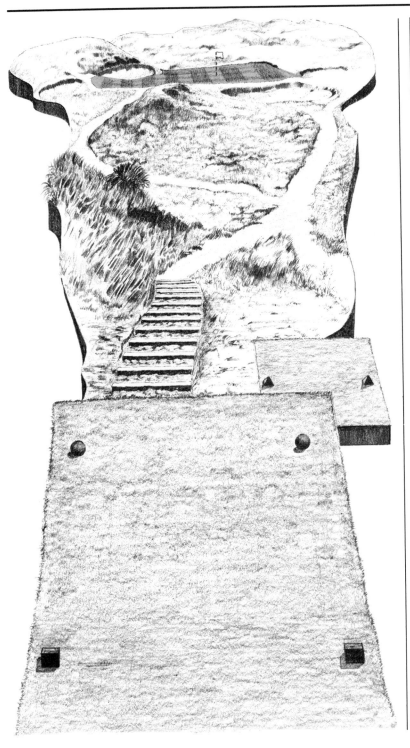

TERM	SCORE TO PAR
Albatross	− 3
Eagle	− 2
Birdie	− 1
Bogey	+ 1
Double Bogey	+ 2
Triple Bogey	+ 3
Quadruple Bogey	+ 4

The scratch player is expected to hit par-3s in one shot, par-4s in two shots, and par-5s in three shots – or regulation figures. If he follows this pattern during the round and takes two putts per hole, which is essentially the par figure on the putting green, he will play to his handicap.

"Okay, Sandy, where does this leave us?" you beginners are, no doubt, wondering.

Par is only your guideline, a reference point. Until you grow into a stronger golfer, capable of hitting the ball longer and of playing all sorts of shots, you probably will not reach every green in regulation. So, you must play within yourself, never taking on more than you can handle.

If you don't think you can reach a green in regulation, avoid swinging "out of your shoes". Playing short and keeping the ball on the short grass is the way to put yourself in position to make a pitch and putt for par – even on a long short hole. If you don't stroke the ball in the hole, that's okay. Bogey is a good score for a beginner like you.

I'll get deeper into the intricacies of strategic play in the next chapter. Right now, for the benefit of you players who have not yet set foot on a course, I'm going to walk you from tee to green, giving you a couple of quick tips along the way.

All holes start on a "tee", a nicely manicured area, where you are permitted to put the ball on a peg – the only time during a round that you will be afforded such a luxury. The Rules of Golf allow you to tee up inside two markers, but never in front, or more than two club-lengths, behind them.

Expect to see three sets of markers on each tee: "championship", "middle", and "ladies". In order, these tees are usually represented by blue, white, and red markers.

On a par three hole, your goal is the green with your first shot. If you miss the green, you'll usually have to play a sand shot, a pitch over a bunker, or a chip from the fringe.

On par fours and fives, you want to hit your tee-shot on the "fairway" – the grass path that stretches from tee to green. On most courses, the average fairway's width is about 50 yards. This may sound like a large expanse of open ground to land a little golf ball, but it really isn't, especially if you try to slug a tee-shot.

Fairways are not always as lush as they look. Occasionally, you'll find your ball in a patchy spot, but don't let a poor lie throw your game out of kilter. Bad lies test you and toughen you up for tournament play. They also encourage you to improvise, and that's a sure way to put new shots in your bag.

Straying from the fairway usually puts you in a problem area – some sort of rubbish that is politely and generically called "rough". When you land in this stuff – usually high grass – you must use common sense and think long and hard about club selection, or else suffer the consequences.

Fairway bunkers, which are basically shallow holes filled with sand and bordered by grass walls, can be bothersome too. Usually placed in the landing area, they can cost you strokes if you don't know the secrets to recovery.

Because rough and bunkers surround a finely cut grass circle, called a "green" (where players putt), an approach must be carefully thought out. Weighing factors such as distance to the green, pin position and wind condition should all be part of your preswing thinking process. If the approach is "blind" and you are unfamiliar with the course, walk up the fairway to see where the putting green is, and keep an eye out for any hidden hazards. If for instance water guards the front of the green you'll have to decide whether to lay up or let it fly.

As to the distance of your approach, American courses have markers, placed 150 yards from the green. Nevertheless, drawing a small map of each hole, with little markings designating how far a particular trap, tree, or mound in the fairway is from the green, will make you a more precise shot-maker, and is one key to being one-up on an opponent, who is visiting your home course for the first time.

Keeping reminder notes on where trouble is and what clubs you hit on par-3 holes, in varying wind conditions or from different tees, can also help you score better. But use your imagination, and devise a detailed booklet that will best service you.

When you reach the green, don't think you can relax. Just because the surfaces look smooth, they are still tricky, featuring subtle undulations. It's just as easy to miss a short putt as a long one, especially when playing a pressure-filled match.

In my career, I have been reminded over and over never to take a short putt for granted. For the umpteenth time, I was reminded of this fact during the 1985 Ryder Cup Match, a biennial event, between British/European PGA Tour players and our American counterparts.

On the second day, I was paired with Bernhard Langer, in a team match against Curtis Strange and Craig Stadler.

Stadler faces a putt, just over a foot long, on the 18th green. If he makes it, Langer and I lose our match, and the American team takes the lead. If he misses (and who is going to think that the best putter on the American PGA

Tour in 1985 is going to miss a virtual tap-in), Langer and I tie our match, and the team score is all-even.

What does Stadler do? Nonchalantly steps up and "stabs" the ball, instead of "stroking" it. The ball never had a chance of going in.

We went on to win the Ryder Cup, but that's not the point I'm making. I'm cautioning you not to rush your stroke, just because the putt is short and the green so beautifully smooth.

Always remember this: all courses look beautiful, but they can turn ugly if you try too hard to beat them into submission. I suppose golf is a little like life. If you hit the ball on the straight and narrow, you'll fare well. If you sway from this route, you'll pay the price.

BEGINNER'S GAME:
BINGLE-BANGLE-BUNGLE

When you start playing golf you can't expect to shoot low scores on every hole. All the same, you want to have fun on all eighteen holes. So playing a game helps stir up enthusiasm among friends. Bingle-Bangle-Bungle is an ideal choice. Here's how to play it.

Three points on each hole. One point to the player whose ball first comes to rest on the green. A second point to the player whose ball is nearest the cup after all players are on the green. The third point is awarded to the player who first sinks his putt.

In settling up, each player wins the difference between his total points and the total points of each player with fewer points.

CHAPTER 19

COURSE STRATEGY – PLAY WITH YOUR HEAD, NOT YOUR HEART

You can have a great technique, but unless you think before you act, and play with your head, not your heart, you'll never accomplish your golfing goals. That's a fact.

Playing strategically is crucial to low scoring, for each course situation sets you up for two "lines" of play. You can either play safe, or, taking a chance, hit the ball along an attacking line.

Off the tee, maybe you must decide whether to gamble and try to carry a burn (leaving yourself a short approach), or to play safe, laying the ball up in front of the water.

On an approach, maybe you have to choose whether to shoot for the flagstick tucked behind a pot bunker, or to play for the fat of the green.

Perhaps, on a 30-foot putt, you must elect whether to charge the ball at the hole (and risk going several feet past, if you miss), or to lag up, for a sure two-putt.

During the course of 18 holes, you'll run into a multitude of situations, some more mind-boggling than others. Your playing capabilities on the day, common sense, confidence, and a constant battle with your ego, will all come into play when choosing the line you want to hit the ball along. You're the master of your destiny, so know what you can and cannot do, what you should and shouldn't do.

Often, the high handicapper stays a high handicapper because he allows his ego to run the show, hitting shot after shot along the attacking line. In the process, he ends up wasting shots, instead of saving them through sensible planning.

In contrast, one reason the low handicapper stays a low handicapper is because he is not afraid to take the commercial line, when he has to. Moreover, when he does gamble, the percentages are in his favour. He makes sure of that. He might attack a pin cut on the back tier of a green, and risk landing in hairy fringe behind, but that's because he has confidence in his chipping game. On the other hand, were there a deep pot bunker behind the putting surface, he would play short of the flag, for fear of facing an extremely awkward lie in sand.

You can see, golf is a lot like chess. Only this time you have to out-think the course by playing strategically. I have one plain and simple philosophy: in your early days of golf, you should take inventory of your strengths and weaknesses, then manage your game accordingly. As you improve, developing more shots along the way, you can start taking more chances.

The longer you play golf, the more sophisticated your game has to become. Strategy will not mean, simply, splitting the fairway with a tee shot, or hitting a crisp iron shot 30 feet from the stick. What it will mean is landing your drive in the best possible place to set up an attacking line into the hole. No more knocking the ball on the green. You'll be looking to "knock the stick down".

Believe it or not, finely tuned strategy also means knowing which side of the green is best to miss on, should the shot not come off.

If the pin is cut left and water lurks left of the green, I'll switch from playing a fade to a draw. At least, then, if the shot doesn't curve back towards the green, I'm chipping, not dropping from water.

I must say, I have learned a lot about this type of play by watching Jack Nicklaus, the master strategist, who never hits a shot until he is sure the percentages are going with, not against, him.

There is a lot more to top-notch strategy, but before reviewing the finer points, I want to introduce you to some of the basics, by seeing just what went through my mind on the par-five, 14th hole, during the final day of the 1985 Open Championship.

Coming into this hole, I was in contention, but time was running out if I wanted to take home the title. The pressure of wanting to bring the trophy back to Britain after such a long lapse of years rested on my shoulders. I tried not to think of that. Instead, I kept repeating the word my father had repeated so many times during my "growing-up" years: "Patience".

This one word prevented me from overreacting and prompted me to take everything in my stride. Although I had played this hole a number of times previously, I tried to think of it as a new hole. After all, in a sense it was, for the situation was not the same as any time before.

At first, the "negatives" came to mind. They always seem to pop up in a big situation. I thought of the out-of-bounds on the right, and knew that if I hit the ball over the boundary line, I was finished. "No, Sandy, think positive," I thought. I did; rather than focusing on where not to hit the ball, I looked down the left side, and knew that was where I wanted to hit the tee-shot.

I made a pretty good swing, and succeeded in keeping the ball away from the O.B. stakes, but I guess the anxiety of the situation caused me to turn my right hand over a little too quickly in the hitting area. The result: a shot that flew a little too far left. On top of that, a bad kick sent the ball rolling past the short rough, into the deep stuff.

The young and immature Sandy Lyle (who did not have a clue about the ins and outs of strategic thinking) would have played with his heart, not his head. He would have been overly aggressive, and tried to hit a miracle shot. Not the new Sandy Lyle. I had learned my lessons, thank you.

I accepted the slightly bad shot, the bad break, too, and got on with business, planning a lay-up shot, short of the renowned water hazard, "Suez Canal".

I didn't even cloud my mind with such thoughts as: "Sandy, you have to make birdie", or "Sandy, if you knock this one down the fairway, you can make birdie, or at worst, par." I thought of nothing except the shot at hand, and if I say so myself, this is the mark of a mature player, who thinks strategically.

To shoot low scores, sometimes you have to bite the bullet and play a percentage shot safely back to the fairway.

The shot was a wedge. I visualised the ball rising out of the rough and landing on the fairway. Then, set up comfortably and correctly, swung, and hit the shot where I wanted to.

Knowing I had used my head gave me the confidence to hit my third shot just off the back of the green, by virtue of a piercing 2-iron into the wind. And pulling that shot off gave me the confidence to knock a 45 foot putt down the hole. I had turned a potential bogey into a birdie by playing strategically. The rest, of course, is history.

Strategic Sense: The Fine Points

Proceeding With Caution

Learning to proceed with caution is one of the key points of strategic golf. Looking at the scorecard and seeing that a hole is a par-4, or par-5, shouldn't be your signal to reach for the driver, especially if the hole doglegs sharply, either left or right.

Sometimes a driver, struck on the screws, will run right through the corner (where the hole curves), and into the woods. If you play a fairway wood, you may leave yourself a longer shot, but you will be hitting from the fairway.

Playing Your Natural Shot

Playing for your natural shape of shot also spells solid strategy. If your average tee-shot flies from left to right, then on most dead-straight, tree-lined holes, you'll want to tee up near the right marker (aiming at the trees on the left), to give your shot room to take shape. If you tee up on the left side, the ball can hit the trees before it has a chance to curve back into the fairway.

Those of you who normally draw the ball, should tee up nearest the left marker and aim at the right centre of the fairway.

Targeting Your Approach Shot

If you want to master the course, selecting a target must be in your master plan. Focusing on a section of the green, up ahead, satisfies your mind as to the type of shot you want to hit.

Picking the right target must be based on the lie and your playing ability on the day. If the lie is good and your game is on form, you might want to gamble and go for the flag. On the other hand, if any doubt creeps into your mind, widen your target to include the "fat" of the green. The latter is an excellent strategy if you face a fairway wood or long iron approach, regardless of how well you're playing.

Choosing the Correct Club

Failing to choose the correct club is a problem shared by many golfers. The basic reason: they don't spend enough time on the practice tee, pacing off the average distance they hit each club in the bag.

CLUB	AVERAGE DISTANCE	
WOODS	MEN	WOMEN
No. 1	220 yards	190 yards
No. 2	210 yards	180 yards
No. 3	200 yards	170 yards
No. 4	190 yards	160 yards
No. 5	175 yards	150 yards
IRONS		
No. 1	190 yards	160 yards
No. 2	180 yards	150 yards
No. 3	170 yards	140 yards
No. 4	160 yards	130 yards
No. 5	150 yards	120 yards
No. 6	140 yards	110 yards
No. 7	130 yards	100 yards
No. 8	120 yards	90 yards
No. 9	110 yards	80 yards
Pitching Wedge	100 yards	70 yards
Sand Wedge	80 yards	50 yards

If you know how far you hit each club, selection is a matter of sheer mathematics. Just subtract the distance of your tee-shot from the yardage of the hole, then choose the club you can hit the remaining distance.

Another factor that comes into play, when selecting a club, is the player's ego. Whenever you try to be "Superman", and stretch a club beyond its limitations, you run the risk of mishitting a shot. If you're puzzled – caught between playing, say, a hard seven iron and smooth six – select the stronger club. This strategy is virtually foolproof; even if you hit the ball over the green with the less lofted club, you'll face a pretty easy chip or pitch, because courses are designed in such a way that the majority of hazards sit on the sides of the putting surface.

One situation that definitely calls for a stronger club is an iron shot to an uphill green. On many occasions, I have had to play as many as two more clubs, due to the steepness of the hole.

Playing downhill shots off the fairway is a different story; if you keep the clubface square at address, you usually have to play one or two clubs less, depending on the ground's degree of slope.

When playing downhill par three holes, always keep the club-face square, and hit one or two clubs less, depending on the tee's elevation.

Dealing With Rough

You'll need to do most of your heavy thinking in the heavy rough.

Think twice before you try to pull off an impossible shot from a terrible lie or attempt to thread the ball through a narrow opening in the trees. More often than not, you are better off knocking the ball out sideways, back to the fairway.

I know following this safe strategy makes you feel that you have wasted a shot. But if you note your score at the end of the day, you'll see it saves you shots. By playing smart from rough, you will usually finish the hole with no more than bogey. Take a silly chance, and you may need a calculator to add up your score.

Dealing With Sand

Hitting into a fairway bunker can be frustrating, especially if you hit the drive solidly. The common approach on a long par four or five hole is to try to hit a wood on to the green. The player is so angry that he ignores the high lip, throws caution to the wind, and instead of making up ground, loses it. Only when the ball hits the lip and rolls back into the bunker does the player wake up. Too late.

If you land in a fairway bunker, play the percentages – a short or medium iron, depending on the lie, lip's severity and length of shot, and put yourself in position to save a score.

Greed won't help you conserve strokes from a greenside bunker, either. If the ball is under the lip, play for safety, not the flagstick, otherwise you'll be hitting another shot from sand, not stroking a putt across the green.

Playing It Cool on the Putting Green

An overly aggressive attitude on the greens can be costly, too. If you face a long breaking putt of, say, 30 feet, try to roll the ball into a two-foot circle around the hole.

Note: If you were to hit a bold putt from this distance, you'd probably run the ball through the break, several feet by the hole, and drop a shot by three-putting.

What's the moral of this chapter? Since no golfer likes to drop a shot to par, by making a silly mistake, know your course and your capabilities.

CHAPTER 20

THE RULES OF GOLF: HAVING THEM AT YOUR FINGERTIPS IS A GOOD RULE OF THUMB

The cliché "Ignorance is bliss" certainly doesn't apply to the Rules of Golf, as approved by the Royal and Ancient Golf Club of St Andrews, Scotland, and the United States Golf Association.

By virtue of my father's influence, I am a stickler for the Rules. He realised early on that studying Shakespeare was not my cup of tea, so he stuck a Rule Book in my hands. "Sandy, read this from cover to cover and you will be a step ahead of the game," was his advice.

On top of this, he told me stories about professionals who had lost matches or medal play tournaments by breaking the Rules.

One clipping he cut out of the newspaper and showed me really registered. In fact, this incident, concerning the renowned Roberto De Vicenzo, still sticks in my mind.

The story goes like this. During the final round of the 1968 US Masters, one of golf's four major championships, De Vicenzo actually completed play with a total of 277, to tie Bob Goalby. However, once the Tournament Committee checked De Vicenzo's scorecard, an announcement was made. There was to be no playoff.

De Vicenzo had lost his chance to capture the coveted green jacket (awarded to the winner of this prestigious event), because he signed an incorrect scorecard.

Tommy Aaron, his playing partner, had marked down a 4 as De Vicenzo's score on the 17th hole, and a total of 66 for the round. Unfortunately, De Vicenzo quickly signed the card without checking his score. The Argentinian had actually scored a birdie-three on the 17th and shot a final round 65.

As the Rules state: "No alteration may be made on a card after the competitor has returned it to the Committee.

"If the competitor returns a score for any hole lower than actually taken, he shall be disqualified. If he returns a score for any hole higher than actually taken (as De Vicenzo did), the score as returned shall stand."

De Vicenzo's new total of 278 placed him second to Bob Goalby.

It goes without saying that I check and recheck my scores today (as you should do every time you play in a competition), freshen up on the Rules and read any new decisions put forth by the game's chief governing bodies – the R & A and USGA.

According to the Rules, no penalty stroke is assessed if your ball comes to rest in such circumstances as casual water, ground under repair or in a hole made by a burrowing animal. But frankly such breaks are few and far between.

If you break the Rules during a stroke play competition, you can usually expect a two-stroke penalty. Commit the same infraction under the match play format, and you'll nearly always have to forfeit the hole to your opponent. All the same, the Rules still help you. If this sounds somewhat contradictory, ponder these thoughts:

Your tee-shot comes to rest in a bush. If the Rules didn't allow you the option to declare the ball unplayable, and to drop free of trouble (taking a one-stroke penalty), you could be swatting at the ball until the cows came home.

I think you get my point: the Rules of Golf are an aid, providing you know them. If you don't, you'll pay a dear price.

Learning all the Rules takes time, but, believe me, the little bit of labour will be worthwhile. Staying up on the Rules saves you the embarrassment of breaking them out of ignorance, saves you strokes by allowing you to drop from severe situations and can stop you from losing a hole or being disqualified.

The trouble is, many club golfers take the Rules lightly by taking them into their own hands during a friendly match. Try to avoid getting into this bad habit, otherwise you'll just be cheating yourself. And during a competition, you'll be cheating your fellow golfer out of a well-earned silver cup.

What follow are ten common course situations. Learn them, and you'll be off to the right start and do the right thing when it counts.

Out of Bounds

SITUATION: Player hits wild shot that finishes out of bounds.

WRONG: Player drops ball back in play, next to the spot where it went out of bounds and penalises himself one stroke.

RIGHT: Rule 27-1: If a ball is out of bounds, the player shall play a ball, under penalty of one stroke, as nearly as possible at the spot from which the original ball was last played or moved by him.

Grounding Club in Hazard

SITUATION: Player's approach lands in bunker.

WRONG: While addressing the ball, player's clubhead touches the sand. He plays on, unaware that he has broken a Rule.

RIGHT: Rule 13-4: Before making a stroke at a ball which lies in or touches a hazard (whether a bunker or a water hazard), the player shall not: b. Touch the ground in a hazard or water in the water hazard with a club or otherwise.

Lateral Water Hazard

SITUATION: Ball crosses margin of water hazard and flies another 50 yards before splashing down in the far side of the hazard, next to the green.

WRONG: Player drops a ball at nearest spot to where it came to rest and penalises himself one shot.

RIGHT: Rule 26-1: The player may under penalty of one stroke; a. Play his next stroke as nearly as possible at the spot from which the original ball was last played, or moved by him; or b. Drop a ball behind the water hazard, keeping

the original ball last crossed the margin of the water hazard directly between the hole and the spot on which the ball is dropped, with no limit to how far behind the water hazard the ball may be dropped; or c. As additional options available only if the ball lies in, touches or is lost in a lateral water hazard, drop a ball outside the water hazard within two club-lengths of (i) the point where the original ball last crossed the margin of the water hazard or (ii) a point on the opposite margin of the water hazard equidistant from the hole. The ball must be dropped and come to rest not nearer the hole than the point where the original ball last crossed the margin of the water hazard.

Bending or Breaking Branches

SITUATION: Ball lies amongst trees and overhanging branches.

WRONG: To make stance and swing less awkward, player bends or breaks branches.

RIGHT: Rule 13-2: Except as provided in the Rules, a player shall not improve or allow to be improved the area of his intended swing or his line of play by moving, bending, or breaking anything growing or fixed.

FOOTNOTE: If these circumstances occur when a player fairly takes his stance, makes a stroke or the backward movement of his club for a stroke, there is no penalty.

Touching Line of Putt

SITUATION: Player about to putt, notices spike marks on his line.

WRONG: Player taps down spike marks with the sole of his putter.

RIGHT: Rule 16-1: The line of putt must not be touched except: for example, (vi) in repairing old hole plugs or ball marks.

Removing Loose Impediments

SITUATION: Player's ball lands on grassy bank, within the bounds of a water hazard. There is a stone behind the ball.

WRONG: Player removes stone.

RIGHT: Rule 23-1: Except when both the loose impediment (natural objects such as stones, leaves, twigs, branches) and the ball lie in or touch the hazard, any loose impediment may be removed without penalty.

Lost Ball Time Limit

SITUATION: Player searches for ball in deep rough.

WRONG: Discovers ball after five minutes have gone by and plays on, ignorant of the Rule.

RIGHT: Rule 27: A ball is lost if: a. It is not found or identified as his by the player within five minutes after the player's side or his or their caddies have begun to search for it.

Unplayable Lie

SITUATION: Player's ball lies at the base of a tree, in such a position that he is stymied.

WRONG: Player tosses ball several yards from the spot, takes a penalty of one stroke and plays on.

RIGHT: Rule 28: If a player deems his ball to be unplayable, he shall, under penalty of one stroke: a. Play his next stroke as nearly as possible at the spot from which the original ball was last played or b. Drop a ball within two club-lengths of the spot where the ball lay, but not nearer the hole; or c. Drop a ball behind the point where the ball lay, keeping that point directly between the hole and the spot on which the ball is dropped, with no limit to how far behind that spot the ball may be dropped.

Moving Ball

SITUATION: Player addresses his ball in the rough, and ball drops deeper into the grass.

WRONG: Golfer plays on, believing there is no penalty because the ball had not moved one complete revolution, forward or backward.

RIGHT: Rule 18-2b: If a player's ball in play moves after he has addressed it (other than as a result of a stroke), the player shall be deemed to have moved the ball and shall incur a penalty stroke.

The player shall replace the ball unless the movement of the ball occurs after he has begun his swing and he does not discontinue his swing.

FOOTNOTE: Rule 18 (Definitions): A player has addressed the ball when he has taken his stance and has also grounded his club, except that in a hazard a player has addressed the ball when he has taken his stance.

A ball is deemed to have "moved" if it leaves its position and comes to rest in any other place.

Waiving the Rules

SITUATION: In a match, a player discovers at the second hole that he has 15 clubs in his bag, contrary to Rule 4-4a.

WRONG: His opponent refuses to apply the penalty. The extra club is declared out of play and the match continues.

RIGHT: Rule 1-3: Players shall not agree to exclude the operation of any Rule or to waive any penalty incurred.

FOOTNOTE: The penalty for breach of Rule 1-3 in match play is disqualification of both sides.

CHAPTER 21

ETIQUETTE – A MATTER OF COURTESY, COMMON SENSE, AND CARE OF THE COURSE

On the golf course, as in everyday life, there is a code of good manners, called etiquette, that you are expected to abide by, if you want to gain the respect of your playing partners and keep golf a gentlemanly game played in a splendid setting.

Courteous golfers, who play at a steady and sensible pace and take care of the course, enable others to think and concentrate.

I guess it's fair to say that golf course etiquette is just as vital as minding your table manners. If you are polite, you will be invited to a friend's for tea. By the same token, if you are a pleasure to play with, I guarantee you will be invited to tee-it-up again, again, and again.

Once knowing how to act in accordance with the code of etiquette became second nature, I started enjoying the game even more. And you will, too.

Instead of wasting mental energy, worrying about whether you are doing the right thing on the course, you'll be able to give full attention to sizing up the shot, setting up to the ball, swinging the club, and scoring.

Etiquette falls into three basic sections: Courtesy on the course, Priority on the course and Care of the course. Unlike the Rules, however, there are no penalties for violations. Nevertheless, if you are discourteous, the penalty might be the loss of friends who have no time for your temper tantrums, gamesmanship ploys, slow play, or failure to replace divots and repair ball marks. I think you'll agree: this loss is a lot more painful than a penalty shot.

To a certain extent, etiquette is about common sense, but it's also about knowledge. So, let's take a brief look at what the experts at the R & A and USGA suggest.

Courtesy on the Course

R & A/USGA: No one should move, talk or stand close to or directly behind the ball or the hole when a player is addressing the ball or making a stroke.

LYLE: When another golfer is hitting an iron or wood shot, stand to his right side, whenever possible, providing he plays from that side. Give him room. Let him know where you are and stay still.

When a fellow player is putting, never stand directly in his line.

Avoid whispering, jingling change, swearing, throwing or rattling clubs and opening the Velcro strap of your glove during a fellow player's stroke.

Acknowledge good shots.

R & A/USGA: In the interest of all, players should play without delay.

LYLE: Be ready to play.

Avoid several practice swings.

Hit only one shot unless you choose to play a provisional ball.

Keep a constant pace in between shots, without walking too

far ahead of playing partners who have not yet hit.

　When it's your turn to putt, be careful not to step on a fellow player's line.

　Move off the green before you record scores.

　Leave your bag, handcart or powered cart at a point nearest to the next tee.

　Never drag your handcart or drive your powered cart over the tee, green or fringe.

R & A/USGA: No player should play until the players in front are out of range.

LYLE: Don't take chances that might lead to injury. Wait to hit your tee-shot or approach, if there's a chance that you might reach the group playing in front of you. If you do make an error in judgment, be sure to yell fore!

Priority on the Course

R & A/USGA: A single player has no standing and should give way to a match of any kind.

LYLE: A single player tends to play quickly, and so rushes the group in front, by staying close on its tail. Or, caught in between groups, a single player holds up play. So, arrange games beforehand or wait until you are paired up with partners before you tee up.

R & A/USGA: If a match fails to keep its place on the course and loses more than one clear hole on the players in front, it should allow the match following to pass.

LYLE: Slow play is distracting and frustrating. If your group is having a bad time on the links, walk to the side of the fairway, well out of range, and let faster players play through.

Care of the Course

R & A/USGA: Before leaving a bunker, a player should carefully fill up and smooth over all holes and footprints made by him.

Through the green, a player should ensure that any turf cut or displaced by him is replaced at once and pressed down and that any damage to the putting green made by a ball is carefully repaired. Damage to the putting green caused by golf shoe spikes should be repaired on completion of the hole.

LYLE: Don't leave course housekeeping to the greenkeeper.

Seeing bunkers raked, divots replaced instead of strewn over the fairways, and ball and spike marks repaired, is aesthetically pleasing and a courtesy to fellow golfers. Clean up after yourself. No one likes to play out of a footprint or have a putt knocked off line by a spike or ball mark.

PART 8

COMMON FAULTS:
CAUSES AND CURES

CHAPTER 22

THE BIG SHOTS – CUTTING OUT YOUR SLICE IS A PIECE OF CAKE

Every golfer should be able to detect a swing fault or, at least, be able to make an intelligent guess why his shots stray. Being able to find a fault and fix it doesn't require the brains of a rocket scientist. You do, on the other hand, have to think logically and have more than an inkling of what a good backswing and downswing feel like.

These days you can watch yourself swing on video. When the teacher says, "There's your fault," you can answer: "Yes, I see, so that's the reason I have been slicing shots." Simple, hey? No way! At least not on the golf course, when you are on your own during competitive play.

Forgive me for sounding so sarcastic, but I still am sceptical about these systems. They really do bug me. I look at them as the lazy man's toy, an easy way out, and prefer the old-fashioned way of "feeling" faults and solving them. Any golfer can see what he is doing wrong on camera, but not enough can solve their problems out on the course, because they

WRONG: Bending your left arm drastically and breaking your wrists at the start of the swing, causes you to pick the club straight up – a fault that spells "slice".

RIGHT: To swing the club on a shallow backswing plane and to coil fully, keep your left arm extended while maintaining minimal wrist action.

fail to "feel" the swing motion.

I have always been a feel player. Keeping tabs on what all the parts of my body are doing when I'm swinging – feeling every action – enables me to trace a fault.

Obsessing yourself with angles of the swing, looking at your technique on video to see if you're doing this or that "perfectly", limits you. It turns you into a mechanical player. And the mechanical golfer thinks so much about swing technique that his body short-circuits. In my opinion, the mechanical man just doesn't make the grade. So wrapped up in the physics of the swing, he usually changes his action from day to day, and gets so mixed up that, eventually, he packs the game in.

This is a sad state of affairs. When the mechanical man finally stumbles on a swing that works wonders, he finds it extremely difficult to repeat it the next day, because he is unable to recreate the precise angles that his superb action is based upon. Had he bothered to play by feel, he would have had a much better chance of sustaining his swing. I hope you are following me, for all this chit-chat about mechanics is critical if you are to appreciate the art of finding and fixing swing faults.

No doubt, you hit shots that feel effortless. I regret to say, though, that the large majority of you probably don't have a clue what you do, specifically, to strike the ball solidly. Here's my point: if you cannot determine what you do right, there is no way in the world you are going to be able to determine what you are doing wrong, when your swing is out of sync.

Feeling the actions of your feet, legs, hips, hands, arms – the role each body part plays – is knowing your swing inside-out. When your swing breaks down, you won't have to ask, "What did I do wrong?" If you know what you do right, you will be able to single out the fault and fix it.

This is the best method of problem solving because it is individualised. The reason you slice may not be the same reason your playing partner hits a violent left-to-right shot.

On the other hand, I accept that there are common faults shared by all golfers. In fact, the purpose of this chapter is to discuss the principal causes of poor shots with the big sticks.

If you think you make the mistakes I mention, incorporate the cures into your swing. But feel each remedy. Then you will have something to fall back on when your swing goes on the blink.

If you are new to the game and, I assume, quite a number of you reading this book are, keep these cures at your fingertips. Even if you become an overnight star, you're still bound to hit a slump. We all do, so stay a step ahead.

The Slice

The slice is the most common shot of club golfers. If you need to be convinced of this, just stand on the first tee of any golf course around the world, and you will see shot after shot fly off course, to the right.

There are several reasons for hitting such a wayward shot. It's too easy to think your setup is open or your grip is weak, although both these positions can lead to a slice. Again, the cause could be due to any one of a number of faults. This is why it is important to know "your" swing.

Most often, the slice is caused by a sloppy takeaway. If you experience such a shotmaking syndrome, you probably break your wrists too quickly at the start of the swing, and thus pick the club up and outside the target line.

The end result of the "pick-up" is a cutting-across downswing action, from outside-to-inside the target line. Instead of the clubface fanning open slightly in the backswing and returning to a square position, it closes going back and finishes open.

Cure

To cure this backswing fault, you must quiet your hands by gripping lightly. This will discourage any abrupt "lifting" of the club, and encourage you to swing your left arm and the clubshaft back in one piece, so the clubhead moves back slowly along the target line, inside a hair, and then up, once weight shifts to the inside of your right foot.

Now, unless you make a major mistake in the downswing, and disturb the natural unwinding of your body, the club will return to a square position, yielding a solid shot that flies down the centre of the fairway.

The Duck Hook

The duck hook is one shot that can cause your score to skyrocket. At least the sliced ball sits down quietly. Not the hook, it runs like a scalded cat, upon landing.

Sometimes, the hook can be traced to hyperactive hands, but usually an overactive lower body is the culprit.

In his travels, the golfer hears the same advice over and over: the secret to power is hip turn. Hence, he falls into the trap of exaggerating the movement by spinning out his lower body in the backswing. His motion becomes so rounded that he looks as if he is swinging inside a giant tea cup. Amplifying lower body action to such a high degree is opposite to what is right, and prevents the upper body from turning properly. And it's the upper body that should take charge in the backswing, not the lower body.

An overactive lower half, caused by the hips and knees rotating quickly, instead of quietly in the backswing, flattens the swing. Thus, the tea cup image. Now, what happens is a negative chain reaction. The wrists roll over so the right palm faces the sky in the backswing, and the club closes by the time the player reaches the impact position.

Cure

To cure this problem, be sure to rotate your hips and knees quietly, as the club swings back slowly. Don't twist them violently. The right move at the start sets off a positive chain reaction. You will make a full weight shift into a braced right leg, coil your upper body, and swing the club up, so that your wrists and hands fold into a pretty package at the top of the swing – in a position to smack the ball with a square, not crooked clubface.

The Sky

The sky is simply a weak shot that flies high. The cause: a faulty downswing.

By now, you know that the lower body's task is to work you and the club back towards the target in the downswing. It is the downswing "boss", just as the upper body is the backswing "boss".

The golfer who hits the "sky" stays back on his right side or fails to transfer his weight back to his left foot in the downswing. Sensing that the club is lagging too much, he makes a desperate attempt to reach the ball by dipping his right shoulder. This instinctive move makes matters worse, not better. Lowering your right shoulder too much causes you to come under the ball at impact. You should be driving the clubface through the ball in the hitting area, to accomplish the sweeping action you need to hit the ball on the proper trajectory with the longer clubs.

Cure

To allow your lower body to lead

the way and unravel make certain that you shift your weight to the "outside" of your left foot, once you initiate the downward motion.

Note: If you allow your left heel to lift high in the backswing, you might want to begin the downward motion by replanting your heel. This is something you can only determine through trial-and-error.

The Top

Hitting a top will cause you much frustration, because as funny as this may sound, you will feel like you made a good swing. But, bingo, the ball either trickles off the tee – a "cold top" – or rolls along the ground.

No, the fault isn't caused by taking your eye off the ball. You top when you fail to stay down with the ball as the club works its way back to the impact position.

"Staying down" is somewhat of an ambiguous phrase, and sticking to this straightforward instruction, to the "T", leads to disaster. It doesn't mean "waiting for the club", by holding back weight transfer and leg drive during the downswing. It does mean to maintain your knee flex through the hitting area and to keep your head behind the ball until after impact.

Knee flex is crucial, for if you straighten up, the club lifts up. Rather than catch the ball with the sweetspot, the bottom of the club contacts the top of the ball. Again, this fault has nothing to do with taking your eyes off the ball. I don't think anyone, except "Superman", ever sees the club actually contact the ball on the drive. To be honest, impact is just a blur, and if you are making a super swing, it will feel effortless.

Cure

The player who fails to maintain knee flex is usually one who sets up with his weight on his heels. If you think you fall into this category, crack your knees down a notch at address, and bend a hair more from your waist.

If you feel your setup is sound, check your grip. You could be holding the club too tightly. This fault will occur if you are trying to "nail" the ball. The fast tempo that you incorporate into your technique makes you lose your balance and lift up in the downswing. Hence: the top.

Working on these features of your swing during practice will allow your shots. to take off *above*, not *along*, the ground.

CHAPTER 23

THE LITTLE SHOTS – SHAKING THE SHANKS IS SIMPLE

Over the years, I've learned to respect the complexities of the golf swing. I realise that even an itsy-bitsy mistake in my setup, backswing or downswing, can cause the ball to fly crookedly off the clubface.

Funny thing is, I can accept errant wood, long, or medium iron shots, more easily than I can off-line hits with the short sticks.

I'm not exactly sure why this is so. I assume it's because the lofted clubs are short, so they should be simpler to control. After all, you stand closer to the ball because these clubs are more upright. You don't have to make a big coiling action of the body because finesse, more than power, is your goal. And therefore the swing should be shorter.

Ironically, I hit as many mishits with the short clubs as I do the long clubs. And although these faults are of a different species, they are no less frustrating.

I tell myself that I'm human, and that I shouldn't expect to hit every short iron crisp, but this way of dealing with the problem doesn't work. Mishits with short irons still bug me, so off to the practice ground I go.

The fact is: no matter what standard you play to, you'll hit the occasional "shank", "fat", "pull", or "thin" short-iron shot. As always, there are several reasons why you can hit any one of these shots, but let's look at the number one causes and the cures for solving the short-iron blues.

The Shank

When you hit a shank, you will know about it. And you will want to put it out of your mind as soon as possible, for it is undoubtedly the most shocking shot in the game. The hosel or "shank" of the club strikes the ball, causing it to shoot off to the right, at a right angle. The strange thing is: if you fear the shank, you will hit one. In trying to get the shot over with, you will make a quick motion, and, presto, a shank.

The cause of the shank, however, is not always traced to negative mental imagery. In fact, this horrid shot most often stems from a faulty setup – aiming your feet, hips, shoulders and the clubface to the right of the flight line.

In actuality, you are set up square to a target that is several yards right of the "real" one. If you were to make a perfect short-iron swing from this address, the ball would float high and land softly, on that spot. But you're not likely to make a perfect swing because your eyes are looking at your *actual* target. Inevitably, your body will make an effort to swing the clubhead down, so that the ball finds that target. At least, it will try to. Unfortunately, it will be a futile attempt, because your address is such that the club swings too far inside the line that extends from the ball to the target. Hence, you are unable to clear your hips, swing your arms freely, and make square clubface-to-ball contact. The best you can do is catch the ball with the club's hosel.

*WRONG: You can make a perfect
backswing, yet pull the ball if you fail to
complete your downward motion.*

*When your left side freezes, your head
locks itself in a static position and your
right side is unable to move into the shot.*

RIGHT: The way to ensure square and solid clubface-to-ball contact is to let your left side lead the downswing.

Once your left hip and knee clear to your "left", your right side can release.

This downswing sequence will allow your hands to follow suit. The left guides the club back to a square impact position, while the right provides power.

Cure

Being blasé about where you point your body and the clubface is a bad attitude, and one that is bound to lead to faulty shots. So, take extra time to set up squarely.

If you have trouble lining up: 1. Pick an interim spot, between the ball and target, and focus your eyes intently on that spot until you jockey yourself into position and, 2. Imagine two railroad tracks running parallel to each other: one track is your body line, the other, the flight line.

The Pull

I'm sure you golfing chess players will agree that the one sensation worse than hearing an opponent say "checkmate" is the sight of a ball flying left of the target.

Most of the time, you probably set up squarely to the ball, make an even takeaway action, turn your shoulders, shift your weight over to your right foot in the backswing and rotate your hips and knees back to a square position, to initiate the downswing, but you still hit the "pull".

Why? You fail to complete your downswing motion by clearing your left hip and knee fully. So, your head locks itself into virtually a static position. What's worse, your right knee and foot "freeze".

Your subconscious senses this: fearful that your body and the club will not move freely through the ball, your strongest hand, the right, takes control.

When your right hand takes over, your left hand can't hold the club square to the target at impact. The result of this right-hand control: the clubface closes, causing the ball to fly dead left. Simply, when the left hand goes left, the clubface goes left, the ball goes left.

Cure

After moving back into your left side in the downswing, allow your left hip and knee to clear to your left. Now your right knee and right heel will release.

When you allow your left side to clear and the right side to "fire", your hand action follows the left-right sequence. Your left hand will lead the downswing and your right will merely go along for the ride, until the exact moment of impact, when it joins your left, enabling you to send the ball straight down the target line.

The Fat

When the clubhead is thrust hard into the fairway, a big fat chunk of turf is thrown up in the air. Thus, the term "fat" shot. The result: a weak hit.

If you suffer from this symptom, take serious inventory of your backswing action. I am willing to bet, in an attempt to swing the club back on an upright plane, you are failing to turn your shoulders.

Yes, you should swing short irons on an upright plane, but this doesn't mean strictly straight up, straight down. If the clubhead follows this overly steep backswing plane, it can do little else but finish up stuck in the ground, unless, of

course, you are a wizard, who can manipulate the club, somehow.

Cure

Just because you are playing a short iron, you still must move the club fluidly and freely along the target line, then inside slightly, before swinging it up.

Although the clubhead will not swing low to the ground for very long, it still has to be swept back, initially, not picked up. This means you must allow your shoulders to turn in the backswing. No, you don't have to make the strong degree of wind up that you would for hitting a driver, but you still have to rotate your left shoulder under your chin. Doing this allows you to swing the club on the proper path and plane and to generate sufficient power to propel the ball the proper distance.

The Thin

The number one reason why the high handicapper hits thin short-iron shots is because he misunderstands the concept of swing path. If you suffer from this low shot that usually flies to the right, you probably have been advised, somewhere along the way, to swing the club from in-to-out. I don't know exactly how this phrase came into being, but it's wrong. If you are trying to match this path, it's no surprise that you "throw" the clubhead at the ball in the downswing, catching it with the toe of the clubface, instead of the sweetspot.

Cure

Let's start by putting you in the picture: the club should swing on an inside-square-inside path.

In the backswing the club moves inside the target line. Of course, this inside path is less flat than the one you swing along when playing the longer clubs, because the short iron is more upright.

Coming down, your left side should clear, making room for the club to swing down the target line, then back to the inside before you complete your follow-through.

To help you get back on track, visualise the path: inside-square-inside. See the club moving along this line.

Then, once you make the proper backswing and start clearing your left side in the downswing, let the swing happen. Forcing the swing by "steering" the club to the outside is never the answer, no matter what club you are playing.

PART 9

PARENTS ON THE LESSON TEE

CHAPTER 24

SWING CHECKPOINTS – BE SURE ALL SETUP SYSTEMS ARE "GO" BEFORE YOUR CHILD SWINGS

We both know that it's in a child's personality to seek attention. Off the course, the child will ride his bicycle with no hands, jump over a high fence, or do tricks with a football.

On the course or practice tee, it's "Daddy, Daddy, watch how far I can hit the ball."

Parents tend to egg on a child, too, with, "Let me see you give it one, Johnny."

I'll wager that you, like me, sometimes fall into the trap of encouraging your child to smash a shot. Don't get me wrong, I'm happy to see enthusiasm shared by parent and child, but if you really want to help your youngster groove the fundamentals of a simple swing, you'll need to spend a few hours on the practice ground, each week, running through a series of checkpoints.

My father used to, and still does, inspect my swing, from all angles. In fact, three times a year, on average, I stay with my family for a few days at Hawkstone Park, and report daily to my father for

what we jokingly call my 5,000, 10,000 and 15,000 mile tune-ups. We take these sessions seriously, knowing how quickly a fault can sneak into the soundest of swings. Since the setup predetermines the motion, that's where the inspection starts.

You, too, should begin by analysing your child's address. So, ask him to take a five iron and align himself to a distant target. Then, go about the inspection as follows.

Place one club across your child's feet and another behind the ball (pointing directly at the target), then move behind your child. This is the best way to check his body and clubface alignments.

If he is setting up correctly, the club across his feet (marking the body line) will be parallel to the other club (designating the target line), and the clubface will be pointing at the target.

If the clubface is aiming left of the target, there is a good chance your child's hands are set behind, instead of in line with the ball, which should be positioned a few inches right of his left heel.

Setting the clubface right of the target is usually caused by keeping the hands ahead of the ball.

So, once your child jockeys his feet into position, setting them approximately shoulder-width apart and square to the target (if they are off the mark), get him to set his hands in the correct position by encouraging him to make his left arm and the clubshaft form a straight line.

Speaking of the hands, the typical child has a strong tendency to hold the club with a "strong" grip, because it gives him a sense of security.

All the same, this is a bad habit, so it's up to you to keep a close eye on the position of the Vs, formed by his thumbs and forefingers. Once you move from behind the child, to a facing position, check that the Vs point midway between his chin and right shoulder.

Don't be bothered too much by the type of grip your son or daughter adopts, just be sure that the back of your child's left hand and the palm of his right are square to the target line. As with all basics,

Reporting to my father for regular swing check-ups helps me keep my technique in tip-top shape.

you must be strict about drumming them into your child's routine, for bad positions poison the swing.

If you try to change his strong grip to a neutral hold, I'm sure he will say, in defence, "But the strong grip feels more comfortable." I agree, it probably does. So, what do you say? Tell him that you know the strong grip feels better, but it's incorrect, and that the more he practises the correct grip, the sooner he will hit more consistent shots. Remind him that the grip is the "engine room" of the swing. If he still needs further assurance, take him to a tournament. I guarantee he'll never see a *top* pro using such a strong hold.

Checking your child's posture is important, as well. Slumping over is common among children learning the game. Again, this position "feels more comfortable". Again, it's wrong. Therefore, it's up to you to stress to your child that standing to the ball correctly (with a slight bend at the knees and waist) is the only way he can give himself the freedom to swing the club on the proper plane and path, and hit the long, straight ball. Once he hears the word "long", he'll wake up.

This type of bad posture can usually be traced to the wrong equipment. However, if you have done your homework, and fitted your child up with the proper clubs, the reason he is slumping is that he's putting too much weight on his toes. Straighten him out. Make sure he puts 50 per cent of his weight between the ball and heel of each foot.

While you're checking your child's posture, you might as well look at his head position. Confirm that your child's chin is off his chest. If not, he'll never be able to coil his upper body by allowing his left shoulder to be pulled under his chin in the backswing. And a powerful turn means a powerful hit.

Be on the look-out for tension, too. Your child's left arm should be straight, but relaxed, and his right arm should be bent slightly, at the elbow. His left arm should be more taut than his right because it should be an extension of the clubshaft.

Once you complete the analysis of your child's setup, remove the alignment clubs. Then, see if his key swing positions are "on the money" according to the following guidelines.

The Takeaway

As your child swings the club back slowly along the target line, then to the inside, using virtually no wrist action, his left knee should be rotating inward, his left shoulder should be moving towards his chin, and his weight should be shifting to his right foot.

First Move Up

Once your child's left kneecap is even with the ball, his left shoulder nearly reaches his chin, his weight shifts to his right foot, and his right leg braces, he should cock his wrists and swing the club upward with his hands and arms.

Position at the Top

Your child's left kneecap should point to a spot a couple of inches behind the ball, his left shoulder should be under his chin, the back of his left hand should be parallel to the target line, and he should be at the three-quarter position of the swing.

First Move Down

Your child's left hip and knee should be rotating towards the target, and then clearing to make room for his hands and arms to swing the clubhead back towards the ball.

Impact

Your child should feel pressure on the inside of his left foot and his right heel should be off the ground. His head should be behind the ball and his left arm and the clubshaft should, essentially, return to the in-line position established at address.

Follow-through

Your child's weight should be on the outside of his left foot, his right arm and the clubshaft should form a straight line (pointing down the target line), and the back of his right hand should be parallel to the target line.

Finish

Your child's belly button should point to the left of the target, confirming that he has cleared his left side, and released his right side so fully that the foot is straight up and down. His arms should be folded, and his hands and the club above his head.

CHAPTER 25

SWING DRILLS – THEY'LL MAKE THE SWING SECOND NATURE

The typical soldier does drill-work until cleaning his rifle, making his bed a certain way, standing at attention, and marching in beat, become second nature. He responds automatically to the sergeant's orders – "About face". "Left-right-Left-right", "Shoulder arms" – without having to think about what he is doing. Daily drills allow him to drum all the movements into his muscle memory. Hence, he operates by "feel". In fact, he could almost do an entire day's routine with his eyes closed.

The golfer whose game is in tip-top shape goes through a similar process. The reason he can face a course situation and choose the right club and play the shot as it should be played, is because he does drill-work on the practice tee. The more hours he devotes to practice, the less he has to concern himself with swing thoughts or technique out on the course. Drills help him keep his swing polished, so that he moves the club, essentially, by feel.

By now you can probably gather that I am a great believer in drills. I'd be a fool if I weren't. Drills helped me learn the basic swinging actions and enabled me to groove more sophisticated shot-making techniques.

Today, drill-work keeps my long swing and shorter strokes

Brushing a forward tee encourages an accelerating sweeping action.

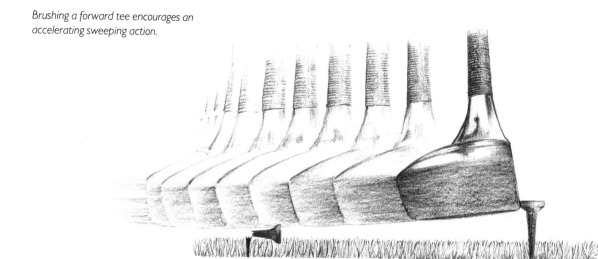

Hitting iron shots with your feet together will help you groove a free-flowing arm swing.

oiled, so each of them runs like a Swiss clock, even when my level of concentration is low.

Drills make practice fun, and practice will allow you and your children to play to a higher standard. Once you can do that, the fun really begins. So, my advice to you and the young golfers in your family: Get to work on the following drills, and the game will never seem like a chore.

Driving and Long-Iron Play

The complete golfer has the ability to hit drives that cut through the wind with a piercing trajectory, and powerful long-iron shots that fly high and land softly on the green.

To put these shots in your repertoire, you must learn to swing on a shallower angle – a sure way to drive the clubhead through the ball after the initial strike, and sweep it off the tee or turf.

DRILL: Place a tee peg in the ground, along the target line, about six inches in front of a teed-up ball.

Swing back, then down, accelerating the clubhead through the ball, brushing the forward tee.

Short and Medium-Iron Play

To become an accomplished short- and medium-iron player, you must swing the club, almost solely, with your hands and arms. Making an uninhibited fluid motion, and not a choppy one, is the only way you'll be able to hit a lofted shot that bites.

DRILL: Address the ball with your feet together and place the ball midway in your stance. Setting up in this fashion will feel awkward at first, because leg action is restricted. But, stick with this drill. It works.

Using a short-medium iron, swing back to the three-quarter position and pull the club through into the finish, with your hands and arms controlling the action.

Cutting a tee in half, during practice, teaches you the art of splashing the ball from sand.

Once you start hearing a swish and hitting the ball airborne, spread your feet normally and incorporate some leg action into your swing. After that, it's a matter of finding a rhythm and tempo that suits you.

Sand Shots

The biggest mistake you can make in a bunker is to try to pick the ball cleanly from the sand. Remember, the key is to pick a spot for the clubhead to contact the sand. If you hit that spot, the sand will lift the ball out.

DRILL: To help you learn the art of splashing the sand, tee the ball up in a bunker, so the top of the peg is even with the surface.

Take your normal address for playing a standard bunker shot, and make a wristy backswing.

Now, swing the club through your spot, trying to cut the tee in half.

Practising this drill over and over will encourage you to slide the blade through the sand. Once you see positive results, you'll start stepping into the bunker with the confidence you need to hit a classy explosion shot.

Chip Shot

Many adult beginners, junior players and average club golfers, fail to hit crisp chips that pop up and roll accurately to the hole, because they break their wrists the moment they start to take the club away. If you suffer from this same fault, you will lift the club straight up and pull it straight down into the turf or the top of the ball.

The idea is to make a smooth, wristless takeaway, keeping the club low to the ground, before you let the right wrist give slightly and swing up.

Keying on knocking a second ball backward (with the head of a chipping club) enables you to ingrain a wristless takeaway action.

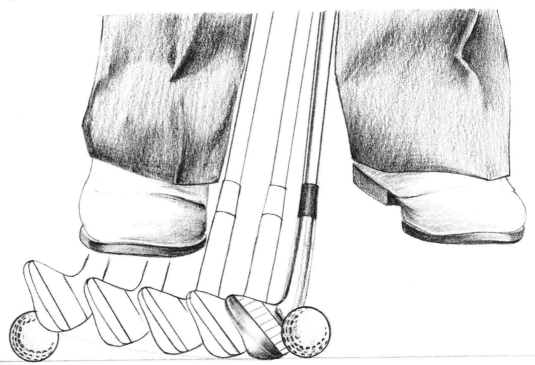

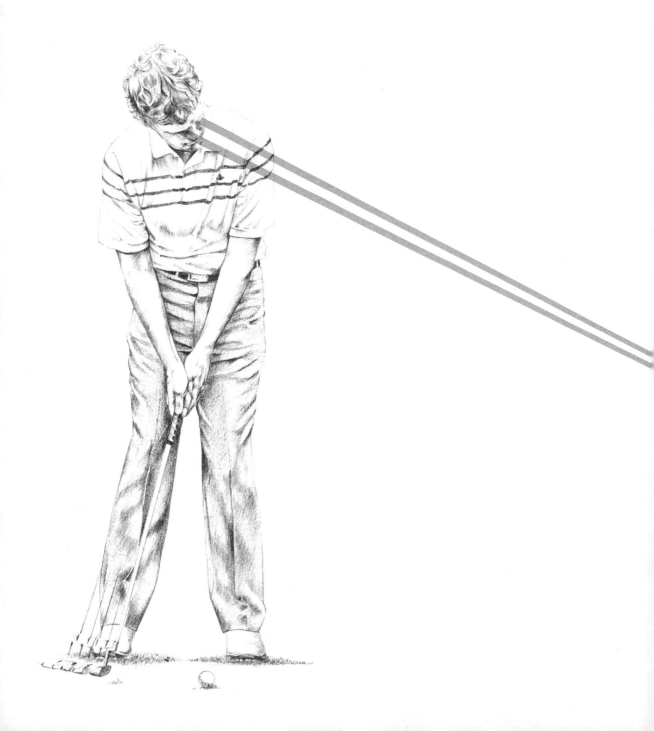

Looking at the hole, while you stroke a long putt, teaches how to lag the ball.

DRILL: Take your normal setup for a chip shot, and place a second ball along the target line, about 12 inches behind the ball you are playing.

Keeping your head steady and eyes on the back of the ball you're chipping, swing the clubhead along the line, just above the ground. If you make a smooth, sweeping action in the takeaway, the back of the clubhead will knock the second ball backward. Incorporate this sound takeaway action into your chip stroke and you're away.

Long Putts

Judging pace is probably the most important key to hitting long putts up to the hole. The problem: the high handicapper looks up before the blade contacts the ball because he is afraid of leaving the ball short. Unfortunately, he usually ends up topping the putt as a result, hitting the ball well past the hole.

I admit, learning the art of lag putting is all about spending hours on the putting green, developing eye-to-hand coordination. Nevertheless, here's a drill that will speed up the process.

DRILL: To help you focus more on distance than the stroke itself, take your normal putting address and set the putterface squarely behind the ball and at the hole, some thirty feet away.

Next, turn your head and look at the hole. Keep your head in that position and make a smooth stroke.

This may take some getting used to, but after a few days of practice, you'll have the confidence to look down and not up, until you've either knocked the ball close from long range, or into the hole!

Short Putts

The golfer who yips short putts makes a quick stab, when he should make a smooth backstroke and accelerate the blade through impact.

This fault can usually be attributed to a mental error in the preswing routine: worrying too much about the line. Break is an important consideration on long putts, but whenever I face a short putt, of, say, five feet, I focus on hitting the ball firmly into the back of the cup, making little allowance for curve.

DRILL: To encourage an accelerating stroke and to get in the groove of focusing on the hole rather than the line, place two rows of tees on the putting surface, as illustrated, and one coin in front, and another behind the ball.

Swinging the putterblade through a narrow row of tees and over a couple of coins, set out on the practice green, will enable you to make one short-pressure putt after another out on the course.

Going back, keep the putterblade dead square to the hole and inside the tees, and try to brush the coin. Do the same going through.

PART 10

PRACTICE

CHAPTER 26

BEFORE THE ROUND – THE TIME TO LOOSEN UP

Many new golfers naively think that smashing balls with a driver is the nature of practice. This is natural, for the "animal" in all of us gives us this urge initially.

I have to thank my father for taming my instincts, early on. There is a good chance that if he hadn't, I'd be beating balls on a driving range, still dreaming of becoming a professional.

One way or another, you will have to learn your lesson, too, or else becoming a low handicap player will remain a pipe dream.

Father educated me, teaching me that practice should be more systematic and cover a wide range of preparation. At the time, I had a hard time accepting this. I feared having to sacrifice the fun of actual play for the sweat of serious practice. Furthermore, his telling me that it would be a good idea not to hit the driver so frequently was the last thing I wanted to hear.

Eventually, I grew up – so much so that, today, I enjoy putting time and effort into my pre-round and post-round practice periods.

However, because I have different goals in mind, these sessions differ dramatically.

Getting Loose

Pre-round practice takes about 45 minutes to an hour, so plan your day accordingly. Arriving at the course with only minutes to spare before it's your turn to tee off, prompts you to pound balls with the driver. This is a sure way to strain a muscle. Moreover, smashing drives speeds up your swing, and rushing, your decision-making process. Starting a round in this state is no way to shoot low scores.

Prior to play, it's too late to revamp your swing. You should be concentrating most on loosening up your golf muscles, although as you will soon see, there are other priorities.

Quite a few of my fellow professionals warm up with a weighted driver, while others swing a few clubs at a time. Swinging several sticks limbers me up, too, except I take this exercise one step further,

and swing left-handed as well, to work my left side.

Touch, Tempo, Technique

Once your muscles are oiled, work on regaining your touch and tempo by hitting a few free-and-easy half-swing shots with the pitching wedge and sand iron.

To get a feel for the steeper action working, move on to full short and medium-iron shots.

To groove the flatter swing you'll need to hit the longer clubs, practise several four-iron shots off a tee. Teeing the ball up encourages you to swing the club more inside the target line, the custom-made backswing for sweeping the ball with the woods and long irons.

Now, progress to the fairway woods and smack a few shots off the grass, before taking out the "big stick". Try not to overdo your driving practice. In fact, if you hit some solid drives in succession, stop. Failing to stick to this Golden Rule of practice will cause you to quicken your rhythm.

If your drives are fading or

Swinging a few clubs left-handed, prior to play, limbers up your left side.

hooking make a quick check of your alignment and grip. If neither of these is the cause of your mis-shaped shots, you'll have to play for the "curves" out on the course. Then tackle the faults in your technique after the round.

Proper Putting Practice

It's a good sign that the majority of club golfers practise their putting so regularly, but a bad sign that they go about it in the wrong way. I don't mean to sound so harsh, but I have to be honest. There is no real value in going once around the putting green, hitting several balls, trying to ram each one into the back of the cup. What's worse is when a player knocks the balls several feet past the hole, picks them up, and walks to the next hole.

The reason I get so frustrated, watching players practise their putting haphazardly, is that I see in them a young Sandy Lyle. I'm only now getting over paying for my poor putting practice routines of the past. And because I don't want you to make the same mistakes, let me put you on the right road.

If you are basically a weekend golfer, your putting stroke is bound to be rusty. The best way to regroove your technique, after a week's layoff, is to follow a simple programme during your pre-round practice.

Putting to the fringe from about 30 feet will help you regain your rhythm and make you better able to judge the pace of putts out on the course.

To work on line and to make your ability to judge pace even keener, stroke several 20-footers at the hole.

Lastly, to develop a short firm stroke for stroking "knee knockers" into the cup, practise uphill three-footers.

After working on these three drills, putt one ball around the practice green, holing out each time, as if the match were on the line. Using one ball forces you to concentrate, because you have no second chance. And, after all, that's what it's like out on the links.

To round off your pre-round practice, hit a few chip shots with a variety of clubs, and a couple of sand shots. Then, you'll be ready to play.

CHAPTER 27

AFTER THE ROUND – THE TIME TO SORT OUT YOUR SWING

My typical post-round practice session is longer and more involved than the one prior to a game of golf. After completing 18 holes, I have a good idea of what I "want" or "need" to work on. If, for example, the forecast is for high winds, I'll practise hitting "wind cheaters". If my putting stroke was sour, I'll try to sweeten it on the practice green.

A poor round can cause much frustration, but putting bad shots out of your mind is not the answer. I understand that, sometimes, you're short of time, due to commitments with friends or family. All the same, if you really want to groove a good swing, keep your short game sound, and become a more complete shotmaker, you must find time to practise.

I accept that it's tough to pick your spirits up following a poor day on the links, and to try to work out your swing problems on the practice tee. Nonetheless, if you grin and bear it, you'll improve.

On the other hand, when you feel "golfed out", you'll do better to pass on practice for a day or so, until you regain some energy and enthusiasm.

If my heart and head aren't into practising, I become so bored that I either try to smack the ball or perform trick shots, such as one-footed drives – two sure ways for faults to slip into the swing. However, I don't put bad shots out of my memory until I have jotted down what I think is causing the problem. That way, I can refer to my notes later on, and iron out my faults.

My basic fault is hooking. If I have an exceptionally bad day of "ducking" the ball into trouble, often I am just not physically or mentally up to post-round prac-tice. I'm golfed out. So, I do what you should do, go home and forget golf. It doesn't really matter how you choose to get away from the game, as long as you do. This way, when you return to the tee, you'll be fresh.

A few weeks before bringing home the '85 British Open Championship trophy, I hooked the ball so badly in the Irish Open that I would have recorded a 90-plus score, had I not picked up my ball in disgust.

My remedy: no post-round practice. Instead, a rest period, followed by a serious session on the tee. When I was ready to con-front the problem and willing to work, I practised hitting fairway wood shots out of a snug lie (squishing the ball down slightly in the turf), for a solid two hours. This drill, created during a meditative moment at home, took

the flatness out of my swing and allowed me to straighten my shot pattern.

If I had practised after that dreadful day at Royal Dublin, my negative attitude would have pre-vented me from being so inven-tive. Instead of buckling down to a businesslike session, I would have hit several buckets of balls and, in anger, probably tried to bang each shot out of the range. Thus, I would have compounded the problem or ingrained new faults.

When you are ready to practise, adopting the right attitude is essential, because swing flaws usually won't work themselves out. Approaching your swing faults in the way that a mechanic looks at the symptoms of a poorly running car – patiently tracing a fault – is the answer. This search-and-solve process will help you get your swing running efficiently again.

The funny thing is that often you will be hitting the ball okay, but without knowing it, a swing fault is sneaking into your techni-que. This is why I report to my father.

In your case, booking regular lessons with your local pro is a good idea.

If you're sure that your swing is in good working order and you've grooved it by hitting full shots with all the clubs in your bag, take some time to practise your short game. Having a friendly competition on, or around, the green, enables you to sharpen up this department.

Experimentation on the prac-tice tee – altering your ball or

To fix an overly flat swing, practise hitting fairway wood shots out of plugged lies.

setup position – can be fun, too. You'll be surprised at the number of new shots you can put into your repertoire through this process of trial-and-error.

Listen to this story, and you'll see I'm not kidding. In the past, whenever I faced about a 30-yard bunker shot, from a buried lie to an uphill green, I was content to get the ball out of the bunker. I didn't think there was much more I could do from such a treacherous lie.

I would step into the bunker, shuffle my feet into the sand, and splash the ball over the top of the lip, landing it on the fairway, but quite a distance from the green.

Since post-round practice is the perfect time to experiment, I decided to do just that. I reconstructed this lie in the practice bunker and making a faster swing, I hit the sand nearer the ball. This technique helped me a little, providing I stayed with the shot. But, quite frankly, I didn't advance the ball much farther than when I used the basic blasting technique. Besides, the gamble of losing my footing or leaving the ball in the bunker was too risky.

At first, I thought, "Sandy, I guess all you can do is wedge it out." But, since I am basically a stubborn Scot, who refuses to take no for an answer, I gave it one last try, using a different club, setup, and swing.

I selected a nine iron, which features a thinner blade than any of the wedges. Playing the ball in the middle of a squarer stance, and using a long and loose swing, worked a miracle. Contacting the sand just behind the ball and driving the thin knife-like blade down and through, sent the ball flying over the lip with so much overspin that it rolled as far as 20 yards.

Getting excited? You should be, for you can learn a lot from post-round practice, if every time you set up to a ball, you have a purpose in mind. Planning your sessions and setting goals makes the time you spend on the tee more refreshing and rewarding.

PART II

STAYING HEALTHY

CHAPTER 28

EXERCISE – STAY FIT TO KEEP YOUR GAME IN SHAPE

I cringe whenever I hear golf referred to as a non-athletic sissy sport. Granted, pro golfers do not have the big and brawny physiques of American footballers, and are not as rough as rugby players, but, on the whole, they are surely athletically built.

If six top Tour players were to challenge six top sportsmen, in contests of cycling, running, rowing, weightlifting and other matches of strength and stamina, I'd be willing to bet that the "swingers" would hold their own against the "muscle men".

There is a very simple explanation as to why circuit pros stay in tip-top shape: they realise that one avenue to playing super golf is exercise. Your key is to follow this same philosophy.

Undoubtedly, Gary Player is the finest example of fitness. At 53 years of age, he remains one of the most flexible golfers around. Although Player is now an official member of the US Senior PGA Tour, he still is capable of beating us youngsters in a proper event –

or major championship! Because there is not an ounce of fat on his body, he is still capable of shooting lean scores.

Player is an example to golfers all over the world. In fact, from the time I decided to turn professional, he has been an idol of mine, giving me the incentive to make fitness a priority in my life. Ever since, I've worked out regularly, at home or on the road.

Sometimes, I find it tough to get up for my exercises and morning run, but reminding myself of the rewards I'll reap psyches me up for my one-hour sessions.

Maybe if I were an all-round sportsman like Jack Nicklaus, whose other "favourites" include tennis and volleyball, I could afford to alternate my workout days. But since I'm basically a one-sport athlete, I repeat my routine each day.

I wish I could tell you that exercise is easy, but, of course, it's not. I can give you a bit of encouragement, nevertheless. The longer you stick to a schedule, the more you will look at this hard work as a

choice – something that you "want to do" – not something you "have to do". Sure, you'll sweat during a session, but you'll also feel super-energised when it's over.

To get you started, I have mapped out the following basic fitness programme for building your golfing muscles. The rest is up to you.

Mini-Lifts

Sitting upright in a chair, with both feet flat on the floor, rest the back of your forearms on your thighs, so your hands hang over your kneecaps and your palms face the sky.

Holding a 5–10-pound dumbbell in each hand, curl your wrists towards you, keeping your forearms flush to your thighs.
Benefits to your body, benefits to your swing
Since this exercise builds stronger wrists and forearms, you'll be better able to make a smooth one-piece takeaway.

Knee Bends

Standing upright, with your feet spread shoulder-width apart, and then squatting down, sounds like a "nothing" exercise, but it's "something".

The secret to getting the most value from this fitness drill is to train yourself to keep your feet planted, as you squat, and then stand back up.

Benefits to your body, benefits to your swing

Regular workouts will help your posture, a key to swinging the club on the proper path and plane.

Your balance is bound to improve, too, allowing you to swing without swaying.

Running

Since running is probably the best exercise for total fitness, I'm not surprised that more and more people are doing a mile or two each day.

Running keeps your heart pumping more blood, with less effort, and, therefore, clears your mental cobwebs. Dare I say, it also allows you to burn up the occasional junk food that we all treat ourselves to once in a while.

If you are not used to running, start slowly by skipping, cycling, or even walking briskly.

Benefits to your body, benefits to your swing

Any of these forms of aerobic exercise will make your leg muscles muscular and springy, so you can drive your lower body in the downswing and accomplish increased clubhead speed in the hitting area.

Running will also help you develop the stamina you need to withstand pressure and to stay strong down the stretch, a big plus if the match or medal is on the line.

Hand Squeezes

One of the best ways to strengthen your hands is to squeeze a tennis ball or even a crumpled-up ball of newspaper.

Benefits to your body, benefits to your swing

Powerful hands enable you to return the clubface squarely to the ball at impact and to hit the ball out of extremely severe rough.

All of these exercises will not only make you physically fit, but mentally tough, too. You'll develop discipline and patience, two characteristics common to all champions.

As to the question of how many repetitions, try to find the number that best suits you. What's paramount is doing each exercise properly. Otherwise, you are just cheating yourself.

CHAPTER 29

DIET – A HEALTHY ONE WILL WORK WONDERS

Making a fluid swing and achieving a firm strike at impact requires a joint effort of mind and muscle. Your brain must plan the shot, while your body must perform the little miracle of working the club back, up, down, and through the ball. Good reason, I think, to stay physically and mentally healthy.

You already know how essential exercise is to playing good golf. Eating the right food also enables you to sustain your strength and maintain mental sharpness over eighteen holes.

As a child, I showed more dexterity with a knife and fork than with a wood or iron. Instead of eating healthily, I filled my stomach with junk food. The pudgy shape I acquired interfered with my swinging action and caused me to feel lethargic after about 12 holes. Consequently, if I were behind in a match, coming down the home stretch, the chances of my catching an opponent were slim, because of the extra fat I carried.

In those days, I felt lousy losing a match due to fat and fatigue.

Even my rationalisation – that Jack Nicklaus was once a big eater – didn't help.

The irony is that in later years, peak performances, highlighted by my '88 Masters win and '85 Open victory, had a lot to do with a switch to a sensible diet. Looking back though, I regret that it took me so long to pay close attention to the food I eat.

Nowadays, eating hearty food does more than help me stay fit. It allows me to make a freer swing, raises my confidence level, and enables me to withstand the pressure of tournament play.

Strangely enough, for the longest time, I was sceptical about dieting. I really didn't think it could make that much difference to my play.

In retrospect, I realise that my reluctance to face facts about nutrition was a copout, because in Gary Player and Seve Ballesteros, to name just two classic examples, I have proof that eating right can help a player "eat up" the course.

In fact, most Tour players are fitness buffs and stay away from

the fatty foods that most people get a yearning for from time to time.

Of course, I cannot design a diet that will suit you. If you are serious about servicing your body, only a nutritionist can help you select the proper menu. What I can do is steer you in the right direction and recommend some foods that will help you stay strong.

If you are anything like me, you will have moments of splurging, but once you see the benefits of eating the right foods, these urges to trade salads for sweets will not come as often. If these cravings should call on you, try thinking of your body as a racing car. Remind yourself that there is no way for your automobile to run fast or efficiently enough to win if you fill it up with cheap petrol. If this strategy fails, and you splurge, just be sure to make small sacrifices the next day.

In the meantime, I hope my eating habits will brush off on you. If they do, I think you will benefit greatly.

Breakfast

I enjoy a soft-boiled egg, slice of toasted brown bread, glass of fruit juice and a cup of tea in the morning.

Another favourite is bran cereal mixed with skim milk, and topped with honey, bananas, or raisins.

NO-NO'S: Big fry-ups and several cups of coffee cause your blood pressure to rise and, thus, hurt your touch around the greens.

Lunch

My midday meals are light. I usually prefer to eat a salad. If I am really hungry, lunch consists of a tuna fish or chicken salad sandwich on brown bread, a bowl of wholesome soup and a piece of fresh fruit. Rather than flush down my food with diet soft drinks, I drink a couple of glasses of tap water or Perrier.

NO-NO'S: Junk food – hot dogs, hamburgers, chips, biscuits, crisps and sweets.

Dinner

After a day's golf I am famished, so I stock up without going overboard, otherwise I am shot for the night and my sleep is restless.

I am a lover of Chinese and Indian food and often sacrifice lunch for a chow-mein or curry dinner.

At home, I have several favourites, including broiled fish, chile, roast chicken with baked potatoes, either plain or lightly buttered, and plenty of steamed green vegetables.

Pasta is a good source of carbohydrates and they are essential to health and energy. So our household stocks up on spaghetti, a dish I enjoy with tomato or clam sauce.

Although I have the occasional glass of wine or beer, I usually stick to water or juice.

My desserts usually consist of yogurt or a mixed fruit bowl.

NO-NO'S: Red meats and high-protein foods do you more harm than good. Excess protein turns to fat and sugar. What's more, it builds fat, not muscle. Too much alcohol will destroy more than your golf game. Creamy desserts are out of the question. My suggestion is to forget dessert, give yourself time to digest your food, and save your appetite for an evening snack of mixed nuts, raisins, or some plain popcorn.

CHAPTER 30

RELAXATION – BEAT TENSION
AND YOU'LL BEAT ANY COURSE

Tension is a major roadblock to playing golf to the best of your ability. When your muscles are tight, you have little chance of swinging the club rhythmically, and this means weak off-line hits.

Unfortunately, if you become uptight, the moment you set foot on the course all the yoga exercises in the world won't help you relax.

The average high handicapper has the potential to play better, yet he makes the same on-course mistakes over and over again, and becomes tense as a result. I want to review his most classic errors, not to mock him, but to teach you a few valuable lessons.

Classic Course Error

The typical high handicap player is pretty conscientious about limbering up before play, yet the moment he tees up the ball, the pressure of actually playing the course gets to him. First, the ball falls off the tee. Next, he fiddles with his glove or hitches up his trousers. Then, he pats his feet up and down as if stomping grapes. Then, he waggles the club in circles, as if cranking up an old Model-T Ford. He settles down, somewhat, but then he's off again, this time making a sloppy practice swing, in an attempt to rid himself of the first tee jitters. More often than not, this practice swing is an unconscious motion, a nervous swat, when it should be a rehearsal of the actual swing.

YOUR LESSON: If you want to beat tension right off the bat, make a smooth, not slow, practice swing, for it's critical that you feel the sensation of the clubhead swishing. If you're unable to get the action just right on the first go, take a deep breath and make a couple more swings, until you find the one that you want to match when the time comes to hit the ball.

Classic Course Error

Tree-lined fairways and hazards also scare the high handicapper. He is so worried about where "not" to hit the shot, that he puts a negative thought in his mind and knocks the ball into trouble.

YOUR LESSON: To relax and get off to a flying start on the tee, put a positive thought in your mind. Pick a spot in the fairway and say to yourself: "That's where I'm going to hit the ball."

Classic Course Error

Another fault the high handicapper makes, and one big creator of tension, is to try to "hit" the ball. He twists and turns his body, jerks the club up in the backswing, and hits down on the ball as if chopping wood. Oh, if he would only swing the club, and stop forcing the swing, he would strike the ball solidly and feel such satisfaction.

YOUR LESSON: If you set up with your body positioned properly to the ball and the target, make a timed takeaway and strong turn, you will not have to worry about hitting the ball. Your downswing

Rehearsing your motion, by making a smooth practice swing, breeds confidence, which in turn breeds relaxation.

will react accordingly, snapping back towards the target, with the club smacking the ball. Square contact of club on ball will be due to a swing, not a conscious hit.

Classic Course Error

When things aren't going well on the links, the high handicapper starts to analyse his swing. The result: mental stress and body stiffness. Trying to think out a picture-perfect swing, the player's self-analysis leads to paralysis. He then makes a quick rigid swinging motion.

YOUR LESSON: If you want to pick apart your swing and work on freezing a certain aspect, such as the takeaway, do this after the round, on the practice ground. If you're having a problem during the round, just picture a good swing. If you have practised, you know what one "feels" like. Now match it.

Classic Course Error

Ironically, when things are going right out on the course, the high handicapper starts worrying about his score, saying to himself, "Now, if I can only go par, bogey, bogey, I will break my record." What happens? His muscles and mind freeze up. So much for records!

YOUR LESSON: If you really want to alleviate tension and play with positive energy, focus on the shot at hand, not the score. If you're in there giving each shot 100 per cent concentration, the scores will come.

Classic Course Error

One more mistake the high handicapper makes is winding himself up in between shots. If he sees his shot fly towards trouble, he worries so much about the horrible lie he must have that he is a beaten man before he arrives at the ball. When the time comes to play the shot, he is a "basket case". What does he do? He hits the ball deeper into trouble.

YOUR LESSON: If you hit a wayward shot, there is nothing you can do about it. Getting yourself all tied up in knots by wondering if you're going to hit a good recovery shot, before you even reach the ball and see the lie, is certainly not going to help you.

So, try to relax as you walk up the fairway, in between shots. Look at the scenery or have a friendly conversation with one of your playing partners.

Besides, if you've practised hitting out of trouble, you can face this shot like a man, not a mouse, and knock the ball on the green. And when you do, put another positive thought in your mind to protect against tensing up over a putt. Tell yourself: "I'm going to make this putt."

Getting it Together

If for some reason you have "one of those days", and walk off the course more tense than ever, do what I do once I leave the locker room and return home to my family: forget about golf. This is a good habit to get into, anyway, for "eating and sleeping" golf can sometimes cause you to lose enthusiasm.

When I'm not playing with my sons or chatting to my wife, I play the handyman, do some gardening, socialise with friends, or listen to music – enjoyable activities that allow me to get away from the golf scene. And when I really want to let my hair down and release the tension, I hop on my motorcycle and go for a ride.

But maybe you are in such a "down" mood about your game that even extracurricular activities don't help you relax. If this is the case, try counting your blessings. Remember you are lucky, that you can go out with friends on a fresh morning and play a game of golf. Lots of people around the world aren't so lucky, for lots of reasons.

If you think about this fact long enough, you'll relax, and enjoy this game for a long time to come.

GLOSSARY OF GOLFING TERMS

ACE: Hitting the first shot from the tee into the hole. Also: hole-in-one.

ADDRESS: The preswing process of setting the body and club in position.

ALBATROSS: Score, on a hole, of three shots under par. Also: "double eagle".

AMATEUR: Person who plays golf as a sport, not as a profession.

APPROACH: Second shot to a par four, or third shot to a par five, usually played with an iron club.

ARMY GOLF: Tongue-in-cheek expression. A golfer plays "army golf" if he hits one shot that flies left, another right, another left, and so on. Thus, the marching lingo: left-right, left-right, left-right.

AWAY: The golfer who is farthest from the hole, or "away", plays first.

BACK DOOR: A putted ball that falls in the "back door" is one that rolls around the hole and when it looks like it will stay out, drops in the back of the cup.

BACK SIDE: The second or "inward" nine holes of a regulation course.

BACKSPIN: Reverse spin imparted on the ball to make it "bite", or stop quickly.

BACKSWING: Swinging the club from the address position to a point above the player's head.

BALL POSITION: Spot where the ball is placed in the stance. Example: opposite the left heel.

BANANA BALL: A wild shot that curves to the right in the shape of a banana.

BENT: A finely textured grass.

BERMUDA: A coarsely textured grass.

BIRDIE: A score of one stroke below the par for a hole.

BLADE ONE: To hit a poor, fast running shot, usually with a short iron, by contacting the ball with the leading edge of the clubhead, or "blade". Also: "skull".

BLAST: Recovering from a sand bunker by contacting the sand with the clubhead, and lifting the ball by moving or "blasting" the sand. Blasting is used synonymously with "exploding".

BLIND HOLE: If a player hits an ideal drive and the green is not visible, the hole is said to be "blind".

BOGEY: A score of one stroke above par for the hole.

BOLD: A shot played too firmly. Usually a putt rolled several feet past the hole.

BRASSIE: A number two wood.

BREAK: The slope or curve in a green when a player putts. He allows for "break".

BUNKER: Pit or depression filled with sand or covered with grass (grass bunker).

BURIED LIE: A ball embedded in sand.

BURN: A Scottish term for creek.

CADDIE: A person who carries a player's clubs and assists him in club selection and strategy.

CAN: To knock a putt in the hole.

CARRY: Distance measured from the place where the ball is hit, to the point it first touches the ground.

CASUAL WATER: Any temporary accumulation of water (such as a puddle), not regarded as a water hazard. The Rules of Golf permit a player to lift from casual water, without penalty.

CHIP: A low shot played from the fringe of the green, with an iron.

CHOKE: To grip down on the club. Also: to crack under pressure.

CLUBBING A PLAYER: To advise a golfer which club to play for a particular shot.

CLUBFACE: The hitting portion of a club, featuring grooves.

CLUBHOUSE: A building with locker, bar, and restaurant facilities, situated near the first tee and eighteenth green.

COCKED WRISTS: The bending of the wrists, during the swing.

COURSE: Land on which golf is played.

CUT ONE IN: To work a high shot, from left to right, so it lands softly on the green.

DEAD: A ball that finishes next to the hole.

DEAD-STYMIED: A player's shot lands in a trouble spot, leaving him no swing.

DIVOT: Slice of turf cut from the fairway by a player's club.

DOGLEG: A hole that curves to the left or right, rather dramatically.

DORMIE: Situation in a match, when a player or team is as many holes ahead as remain to be played. Opponent(s) must win every remaining hole(s) to tie the match.

DOUBLE BOGEY: A score of two over par for a hole.

DOWN: The number of holes (match play) a player is behind an opponent. Also: Ball sitting "down" in grass.

DOWNSWING: Swinging the club from the top of the swing, to impact.

DRAW: A shot that flies with a slight curve, from right to left.

DRIVE: To hit a ball from a tee, usually with a number one wood.

DUB: Barely hitting the ball. Also: "stub".

DUCK HOOK: A low shot that starts its flight left of the target line, and flies farther left, hitting the ground quickly.

DUFFER: An unskilled player or "hacker".

EAGLE: A score of two strokes under par, for a hole.

FADE: A ball that flies on a slight curve, from left to right.

FAIRWAY: The mowed area of the course, between the tee and the putting green.

FAT: Weak shot that occurs when the club digs deep into the turf, behind the ball. A fat chip is called a "chili-dip".

FIELD: All competitors in a tournament.

FINISH: The final part of the swing, when the club moves upward again.

FLAGSTICK: A movable pole placed in the hole to show its location on the green.

FLANGE: Additional surface of the clubhead which protrudes at the bottom or "sole".

FLIER: A ball that flies without spin, so goes farther than normal, because of wet grass or moisture on the clubface.

FOLLOW-THROUGH: Driving the clubhead through the ball, after the moment of impact.

FORE: Warning cry to persons in danger of getting hit by a ball.

FORECADDIE: A person employed by a tournament committee to spot and mark balls, especially on blind holes and in areas of heavy rough.

FOUR-BALL: A match in which two golfers play their better ball against the better ball of two opponents.

FOURSOME: A match in which two play against two, and each team plays one ball. Format: alternate shots, alternate tee-shots. Also: four golfers playing together.

FRINGE: Low-cut grassy area immediately surrounding a green.

FRONT SIDE: The first or "outward" nine holes on a regulation course.

GIMME: In match play, a putt so short that it is usually conceded by an opponent. Not allowed during stroke play competition.

GRAIN: The direction grass grows on a putting green.

GREEN: Flat low-cut surface that players putt on.

GREEN FEE: Money paid for the privilege of playing a course.

GRIP: The part of the shaft covered with rubber or leather, by which the club is grasped.

GROSS: Total number of strokes on a hole or course, before a player's handicap is deducted.

HALVED: In match play, a hole or game is "halved" when two players, or teams, tie.

HANGING LIE: A ball that rests on an extreme downhill slope.

HAZARD: Bunker or body of water, on a golf course.

HEAD: Part of the club with which the ball is struck, consisting of the neck, heel, toe, sole, and face.

HEEL: Part of the clubhead nearest the shaft. Also: a shot that flies left, due to the heel of the clubhead contacting the ball.

HOLE: A round receptacle in the green, four and one quarter inches in diameter, at least four inches deep, and usually metal lined.

HOLE-HIGH: A ball finishing even with the hole, off to one side.

HOLE-OUT: Knocking the ball into the hole, from anywhere on the course.

HOME: The green.

HONOUR: Privilege of hitting first from the tee. Accorded to the winner of the previous hole.

HOOK: Shot that veers sharply from right to left.

HOSEL: The hollow part of an iron clubhead, into which a shaft is fitted.

IMBEDDED BALL: Ball buried in soft or wet turf.

INSERT: Part of the clubface of a wooden club.

IN-THE-LEATHER: In a friendly match, a player will usually concede a putt that lies no farther from the hole than the length of the leather wrapping on a putter.

LAG: To hit a long putt with the intention of leaving the ball close to the hole.

LATERAL HAZARD: A water hazard that runs approximately parallel to the line of play.

LIE: Position in which a ball rests on the ground. Also: the angle the shaft makes with the ground, when the club is soled, or sitting in the natural position.

LIP: The rim of the hole, or bunker.

LOFT: Degree of pitch built into the clubface and designed to lift the ball into the air.

MAKING THE TURN: When a player completes the front nine and moves on to the 10th tee.

MATCH PLAY: Competition by holes. Example: player A beats player B on the first hole and goes one-up. They tie the remaining holes. Thus, player A wins one-up.

MEDAL: Competition of stroke play format. Player adds total scores for 18 holes.

MULLIGAN: A try-again shot, usually off the first tee. Common only in friendly matches, but illegal according to the Rules of Golf.

NAIL-ONE: To hit the ball hard and far.

NECK: The part of a wooden club – where the shaft joins the clubhead.

NET: A player's score, once his handicap is deducted.

ON THE SWEETSPOT: Hitting the ball dead-centre on the clubface. Also: "on the screws".

OVERCLUBBING: Hitting too much club. Example: playing an eight iron when the shot calls for a nine.

PAR: The number of strokes an excellent player should take for a hole.

PASS: In the downswing, the movement of the lower body through impact.

PENALTY STROKE: A stroke added to a player's score for violating the Rules.

PITCH: Approach shot hit with a lofted club, usually a pitching wedge. Ball flies high and stops quickly.

PITCH-AND-RUN: A short-pitch shot that flies low, lands and rolls up to the flag.

PLAYING THROUGH: A group of players given permission to pass a slower group, playing ahead.

POT BUNKER: A deep sand trap.

PROVISIONAL: A ball played after a previous shot is believed to be lost or out of bounds.

PULL: A ball that flies left of the target, with little or no curving action.

PUNCH: A low controlled shot, played with a shorter swing.

PUSH: A ball that flies to the right of target with little or no curving.

PUTT: Stroke made on the green with a putter.

RUB OF THE GREEN: This occurs when a ball in motion is stopped or deflected by an outside agency. Whether the result goes for or against the player depends on the element of luck.

SANDBAGGER: An adept golfer who plays well below his handicap when money is on the line.

SCRATCH: A player who receives no handicap allowance.

SHAFT: The part of the club which is not the clubhead.

SHANK: Golf's ugliest shot. This occurs when the hosel of the club or shank contacts the ball, causing it to shoot dead right. Also called a "socket".

SINGLE-FIGURE PLAYER: A golfer with a handicap of 1–9. Also: low-handicapper.

SKY: A very high shot.

SNAKE: An extremely long putt that winds back and forth over several undulations in the green.

SOLE: The bottom of the clubhead. Also, grounding the club at address.

SOLE PLATE: The metal plate located at the bottom of a driving club.

SPRAY: To hit the ball wildly.

STANCE: Position of a player's feet when he addresses a ball.

STROKE HOLE: Hole(s) at which a player applies a handicap stroke. The scorecard designates stroke holes.

SUDDEN DEATH: Tied matches are broken by a sudden-death playoff – the continuation of a match or stroke play competition ending as soon as one player wins a hole.

SUMMER RULES: Golfers play ball as it lies.

SWING: The action by a player in stroking the ball.

TAKEAWAY: The start of the backswing. When the player moves the clubhead low to the ground.

TEE: A peg on which a ball is placed. Also, the teeing ground.

TEXAS WEDGE: A shot played from off the green, usually from a low-lipped bunker or the fringe, with a putter.

THREAD THE NEEDLE: Hitting a shot through a narrow opening.

TOE: The part of the clubhead farthest from where it joins the shaft. Also: to hit the ball to the right, by contacting it with the "toe" of the club.

UNDERCLUBBING: Using a club that will not reach the green. Example: hitting a nine, when the shot calls for an eight.

UNPLAYABLE LIE: A ball in such an awkward position that the player chooses to take relief.

UP: In match play, the number of holes a player is ahead of an opponent. Also: ball sitting "up" in grass.

WAGGLE: The preliminary movement of the club or the body, prior to the actual swing.

WHIFF: Missing the ball.

WIND CHEATER: A low-hit ball that pierces a headwind.

WINTER RULES: A ball lying on any "closely mown area" through the green may, without penalty, be moved or may be lifted, cleaned and placed within six inches of where it originally lay, but not nearer the hole.

YIP STROKE: A nervous jab of the putterblade on the ball.

SANDY LYLE
PROFILE

SANDY LYLE PROFILE

Born: 9.2.58 Shrewsbury, England.
Height: 6′ 1″
Weight: 180 pounds
Family: Sons – Stuart and James
Turned professional: 1977

AMATEUR VICTORIES

British and National Union Championships

1975 1977
English Amateur Stroke Play

Major Amateur Tournaments

1977
Berkhamsted Trophy

1977
Berkshire Trophy

1977
Hampshire Hog

1977
Scrutton Jug

1975
Carris Trophy

1974
County Champion of Champions

Regional and County Championships

1976
Shropshire and Hereford Amateur

1975
Shropshire and Hereford Amateur

1975
Midland Open

1974
Shropshire and Hereford Amateur

1974
Midland Amateur

Junior Titles

1977
British Youths

1977
Youth International

1976
Youth International

1975
Youth International

1975
Boy International

1974
Boy International

1973
Boy International

1972
Boy International

International Representation

1977
Walker Cup Team

1977
England (Home Internationals)

1977
England (European Team Championship)

1976
England (Home Internationals)

1976
GB vs. Europe

1975
England (Home Internationals)

1975
GB Commonwealth Team

Sandy Lyle represented England at boy, youth and full international level in 1975.

PROFESSIONAL CAREER VICTORIES

1988

Phoenix Open

Greater Greensboro Open

U.S. MASTERS TOURNAMENT

Dunhill British Masters

Suntory World Matchplay Championship

1987

Tournament Players Championship

German Masters

1986

Greater Greensboro Open

1985

OPEN CHAMPIONSHIP

Benson & Hedges

Nissan Cup World Championship (Hawaii): Individual
winner

1984

Kapalua International (Hawaii)

Casio World Open (Japan)

Hennessy-Cognac Cup (Individual winner)

Lancôme Trophy

Italian Open

1983

Cepsa Madrid Open

1982

Lawrence Batley International

1981
Lawrence Batley International
Paco Rabanne French Open

1980
Coral Classic
World Cup (Individual winner)

1979
British Airways/Avis Open (Jersey)
Scandinavian Enterprise Open
European Open
Scottish Professional

1978
Nigerian Open

1977
PGA European Tour School – Low qualifier

International Appearances
Ryder Cup Team: 1979, 1981, 1983, 1985, 1987
Dunhill Cup Team (Scotland): 1985, 1986, 1987
Kirin Cup Team: 1985, 1986, 1987
World Cup Team (Scotland): 1979, 1980, 1987
Great Britain vs. Europe: 1980
Hennessy-Cognac Cup: 1984

MISCELLANEOUS HIGHLIGHTS
Vardon Trophy: 1985
Low World Stroke Average: 1984 (105 rounds played;
70.00 stroke average).
Vardon Trophy: 1980
Vardon Trophy: 1979
Frank Moran Trophy: 1979
Rookie of the Year: 1978

PGA European Tour Order of Merit Standings

YEAR	MONEY	STANDING
1988	234,990	5
1987	245,355	12
1986	110,990	24
1985	199,020	1
1984	110,370	4
1983	61,020	5
1982	86,141	2
1981	51,265	3
1980	66,060	1
1979	49,232	1
1978	5,233	49

Money in Pounds Sterling.

Worldwide Earnings

YEAR	MONEY	STANDING
1988	1,182,438	4
1987	767,891	4
1986	337,570	44
1985	468,823	10
1984	374,522	18
1983	115,039	88
1982	160,209	40
1981	117,671	59
1980	194,881	21
1979	118,411	43

Money in U.S. Dollars.

* In 1988 Sandy Lyle climbed to the number 3 spot in the prestigious SONY World Ranking. Lyle's status was boosted by a strong 7th place finish on the U.S. PGA money list, which earned him $726,934.